RELIGION AND RABINDRANATH

RELIGION AND RABINDRANATH

MOHIT CHAKRABARTI

PUBLICATIONS
KALPAZ PUBLICATIONS
DELHI-110052

Religion and Rabindranath

Rs. 630

ISBN: 81-7835-616-3

Published in 2008 in India by
Kalpaz Publications
C-30, Satyawati Nagar,
Delhi-110052
E-mail: kalpaz@hotmail.com
Phone : 9212729499

Lasser Type Setting by: Rudra Computer Graphics, Delhi
Printed at : Singhal Print Media, Delhi

Professor Karuna Sindhu Das,

Vice Chancellor,

Rabindra Bharati University, Kolkata

and

Professor Abdul Mannan,

Vice Chancellor,

East-West University, Dhaka, Bangladesh

Contents

Preface

Religion is what prompts and accentuates one towards continual ascent and excellence. It is a *vrata*—a devotion and dedication par excellence—to be in perfect fusion with the All Best and All Serene inherent in oneself. To Rabindranath Tagore, religion is what one ought to be from what one is in order to be justified to the intrinsic vision of fullness and truth. 'The truth of the Eternal Man' as he conceptualises *dharma*, points to the spontaneous efflorescence of one who aspires after being religious to expand and explore the unending horizon of humankind. From the conceptual points of view, he, therefore, places man as the focal point of religion encompassing truth, joy, love and other essential components of religion that profusely contribute to the poignancy and perfection of man as the embodiment of the All Serene. "Conceptual Framework of Rabindranath's Religious Philosophy" extensively deals with these ends-in-view.

"Religion and Functions and Festivals: Tagorean Quest" is an in-depth study of how Tagore makes and directs religion as one's very way of life sensible, meaningful and practical in day-to-day activities. In fact, he explores a new dimension of religion in manifold visions—aesthetic, mystic and spiritual in particular—

which find apposite manifestations in observations of diverse functions and festivals which are closely related to man and society. To be at one with God—*Yuktatmanah*—or to be peaceful—*prasantah*—in order to be a perfect representative of the All Serene always awaits a sincere and sustained association with functions and festivals which, as Tagore always introduces in Visva-Bharati, welcomes us to have a warm and cordial entry into the cathedral of religion.

Unlike any other religious visionaries, Tagore synchronises religion with joy. 'The indwelling light of truth' as he elucidates joy always allows one to look within and to look in eternal poignancy and askance to unfold the vision of the All Serene within oneself. He delves deep into the world of joy with the firm conviction that the world with all its creations signifies the re-birth of man in the religion of joy that allows freedom to be a constant partner to encounter the All Serene. "Religion and Joy: Tagorean Synchronisation" reveals Tagore's vision of joy as the inseparable and abiding factor of religion in the true sense of the term.

An incomparably refreshing and life-enriching religio-humanist, Tagore glorifies man as the endless seeker of the Man of the Heart—*Maner Manush*—whom he also christens as *Pathbhola Pathik*—a Waylost Traveller. "Religion and Humanism: Tagorean Depth of Vision" is an elaborate analysis of how Tagore explores the spirit of the best in one in association with the *Parama Purusha,* the Person Supreme, so much so that the symphony of religion and humanism becomes a living reality in poignancy and purity as the image of the All Serene.

A quest for the essentials of excellence always prompts one to be in perfect tune with religion. Spirituality stands for that excellence and waits for a perfect fusion with religion. Tagore probes deep into the essentials of excellence in religion wedded to spirituality. "Religion and Spirituality: Tagorean Essentials of Excellence" is a penetrating analysis to justify these ends-in-view.

"Religion and Creativity: Tagorean Vision of Serenity" and "Religion and Mysticism: Tagorean Beyondings" may evoke newer avenues of erudition and enquiry into the Tagorean thoughts and experiments on religion.

To extend the altruistic vision of the society in terms of religion and vice versa is an arduous task. As Tagore believes in religion as an evolution of all-round consciousness, he extends the canvas of religion as realisation of oneself in each and all and advocates for cultivation of personality best suited to highlight the spirit of 'I am' to 'Thou art' as the image of the All Serene. His vision of *Yuktamanav,* a fusion of the individual and the Divine Self, for the well-being of the society crystallised in Truth, Beauty and Goodness signals a new religion of man yet to be translated in the society. "Religion and Society: Tagorean Perspectives" is an earnest scholastic endeavour towards this direction.

"Religion and Education: Tagorean Synthesis" may significantly draw the attention of anyone interested in the aims and objectives of education in terms of religion and vice versa and re-orientation of these aims and objectives as Tagore thinks and experiments in his own educational institutions at Visva-Bharati.

To explore and expand a religion of religions is to explore and expand a religion par excellence, a religion that beckons an ever enlightened evolution of man. "Towards a Religion of Religions: Tagorean Forethoughts" may initiate us to be baptised in the vision of religion of joy and love, truth and humility, dedication and devotion, promise and perfection.

I gratefully recall the warmth of sincerity in the computer processing of the book by my son, Sobdo Chakrabarti.

I would also like to express my profound reverence to Professor Karuna Sindhu Das, Vice Chancellor, Rabindra Bharati University, Kolkata and to Professor Abdul Mannan, Vice Chancellor, East-West University, Dhaka, Bangladesh. I dedicate my book to them as a token of gratitude.

To be in tune with Tagore is to be in the best tune with religion. If the book appeals to every revered reader interested in the religion of Rabindranath Tagore, I would serenely recall: 'a feeling of tremulous joy is passing through my heart'.

'Seemantika'
Seemanto Palli
Santiniketan-731 235
INDIA

Mohit Chakrabarti

1

Conceptual Framework of Rabindranath's Religious Philosophy

Religion as Rabindranath Tagore conceptualises is an eternal efflorescence and excellence of man. It is an ascent ceaseless and, therefore, thrilling of what one is to one ought to be in all endeavour and sincerity, devotion and dedication, humility and serenity. It is an endless expansion of the little self to be in perfect unison with the Divine or the Supreme Self in every human being. It is a halo of all haloes with all magnificence and grandeur, solemnity and order. It negates all littleness and, like light eternal, spreads its vastness in the universe where the unending horizon of humankind simply expands with all aura of illuminations by being blessed with the vision of the All Serene.

Tagore never admits religion with slightest obscurity and ambiguity, abstraction and inaccessibility. He never wants it to be fathomed and fashioned in pedantic poses and robes but highlights it with all simplicity and fullness, clarity and poignancy. As a practical visionary, he draws our attention to the worldly mockeries and sentimentalism of entangling religion in all littleness of day-to-day life so much so that the essence of religion inherent in simplicity and broadened vision of life is throttled in vagaries of emotion and vested interests. The constraints thus created in irreligion or de-conceptualising religion become a breeding ground for feuds among castes and communities, parties and groups professing different opinions and ideologies about religion. That such type of utilisation of religion as one aspires drags it down to pettiness and meaningless abstraction is what Tagore wants time and again to draw our attention in order to make a strong vigil against all ukase.

Admittedly, religion thus denied a spontaneous and simple efflorescence in the heartland of humanism has greatly pained Tagore. He categorically points out to the fact that we are yet to accept and translate religion heart and soul. This has actually created a vast difference between what we think and what we actually perform in the name of religion. We dwarf the vastness of religion by weighing it in the balance of our vision about its practicability in accordance with our whims and caprices, little wills and aspirations. When religion comes down to the level of the fulfilment of one's wishes and aspirations of littleness, it loses its best essentiality, the touchstone of one's excellence and ascent with all promises of the beyonding of man.

Tagore explains religion as an effulgence of the endless joy one feels, appreciates, wishes and encounters in one's own mind. Unless the mind is in unison with endless joy, religion loses its proper identity and favours communalism, sectarianism, fundamentalism etc. where joy is derived from narrow and irreligious objectives. Joy then comes down to the level of fulfilment of petty emotional sensibilities and sentimental ends-in-view. It is also dwarfed in vested idealism where society is more interested in utilitarian objectives than altruism and fights shy of serenity of vision which is the foundation of true religion.

Unlike western religion, Indian religion as Tagore asserts is never a quest for what virtue is and what is vice. Indeed, it is a quest for endless joy—a quest in the midst of living one's life in a disciplined manner. What is that discipline? Tagore's answer is very categorical. He refers to continual and sincere cultivation of pure and unalloyed simplicity of the mind controlled and crystallised in all earnest endeavour. But, then, control of the mind in order to practise simplicity to have the essence of religion is not an easy affair. It requires ceaseless practice of poignancy and performance of at least two other components which Tagore considers invaluable. These are happiness and contentment which are the fruits of control of the mind. In fact, any quest for religion at its best should make an unending journey onward to cultivate simplicity by means of restraint of the mind to be blessed with one prized goal of joy that stands for religion as its best identity.

To understand and appreciate religion in its true perspective, the two-way process of arriving at or having joy from contentment, happiness and simplicity or starting from the former to investigate the latter introspectively is a limitless and, therefore, pulsating vision of life. The constant signal that one receives within the course of making such an exercise is to verify if one is really trying to be awakened, to be effulgent, to be consolidated or stabilised in order to be justified to the invaluable quality of simplicity. Unless this exercise of inwardness to oneself in quest of the simplicity of religion is made, religion suffers from absence of finer aesthetics and nobler ideals for which it naturally stands.

Tagore reminds us time and again that true religion is always a pointer to one's contentment received from the world of joy. But this joy as he rightly remarks must be the offspring of unending and crystallised sense of restraint in one's thoughts and contemplations. It is something like the quest of an individual in the lotus-land of the mind for contentment born not of one's own desires and aspirations but of sacrificing one's own desires and contemplations for the well-being of others.

Santoshang hridi sangsthaya sukharhi sanyato bhavet—one who craves for happiness should be restrained by placing contentment upon one's heart. Tagore warns against irreligion bred in ukase and turmoil of the mind in restlessness in search of contentment only by a superficial quest for happiness where no crystallisation of one's contemplation actually takes place. And whatever is exercised in the name of contemplation becomes a crazy component of religion sans purity sans simplicity.

Again, with western religion, taking the lead role as an exponent of the values of life does not appeal to the conscience of Tagore who never allows religion to be belittled as a narrow force engineered for an ethical and moral vehicle of enquiry. Humankind as he sincerely feels, sustains and disseminates, eyes and accentuates religion not in terms of narrow moral and ethical fulfilment of objectives but in some more important and broader ends-in-view of fullness of human growth and development. In fact, when he upholds religion as an exponent of Truth, he encapsulates joy and love together which stand for the All Great. How does it appeal in the forms of love, truth and joy as he synchronises all these in religion? He gives a very categorical, straightforward, pointed and poignant answer. All endeavour of joy, for example, should be enriched with grandeur, beauty and affluence not only simply extrinsically but also principally and, of course, serenely intrinsically. The grandeur of joy derived from religion as such accelerates the vision of fullness of One All Serene as existent in one's own self all the time. The beauty of joy in religion has its lustre not in crudity but in simplicity which is actually the affluence of joy that vitalises the essence of religion. As for oneself in quest of true religion, Tagore highlights the Indian approach to religion where one is christened with the spirit of making an endearing kinship with the whole universe—*Vasudhaivakutumvakam*—thus enlarging the vastness of the human heart pining for universal kinship with the One in oneself by endearing the One in all.

The concept of religion as Tagore manifests in his concept of Brahma shows how he adroitly reveals the vision of the All Serene as embodied in every human being. He makes a fusion of work, sight, sound and thought in humankind by confirming the fact that the All Serene is Omnipresent and at the same time Omniscient. He goes further in elucidating that Brahma is actually the Life of every life, the Heart of every heart and the Mind of every mind. He also highlights Brahma as the Eye of all eyes. Therefore, the person who professes or practises religion par excellence is always ready to sacrifice himself for the cause of Brahma in order to be blessed with fullness.

With full faith in the invaluable words of the Upanishad—*Satyam Jnanam Anantam Brahma* – Tagore entrusts religion with the poignancy of vastness in erudition and truth for which the eternal quest of mankind never allows surrender to manifold constraints. It is that religion which embraces joy in the midst of sorrow, discipline in the midst of sorrowful ukase and courage amidst all untoward and horrible circumstances. Elucidating the concept of humanism from the perspective of religion as he crystallises in day-to-day constraints in all forms, he represents religion as an unending fountain of joy. In his own words:

> Many a time it may be a matter of comfort for us, which brings forth our dwarfishness and paucity, but it is not a matter of joy for us. The one which we receive not by heroism, nor by tears, which can be had easily and, therefore, we do not receive in fullness—the one which we receive in all difficulties in course of sorrow, our hearts only receive that in all totalities intensely. Humanism is the wealth of our great sorrow. That can be achieved by means of heroism alone. If that would not have been achieved by overcoming constraints at every step everyday, then we would not have achieved even by achieving that—if that was cheaply available, then our hearts would not have whole-heartedly accepted that. But that is easily available either by sorrow or by fear from death, either by fear and danger or by multi-dimensional emotional traits. With a view to making an endeavour to achieve this rare humanism, the soul begins to feel all its strength. His real joy lies in that very feeling. In it alone he does bear his own identity. In it

alone he can know that his head is above sorrow, his initiation is above death.

—Rabindranath Tagore: *Dharma* (Religion), *Rabindra-Rachanavali* (Collected Works of Rabindranath Tagore), Government of West Bengal, Calcutta, 1992, Vol. XIV, pp. 584-585.

[Translated by me]

The concept of religion in realisation of One as the All Serene holds the key to Tagore's religious vision. The truth of One also holds the joy of One, the fearlessness of One and the unending grandeur of One to adorn the dissociated world with boundless aura of beauty. Religion thus conceived in One as the exponent of the All Serene also manifests the four-fold dimension of Tagore as a religious visionary:

(a) The beautiful One is a great creation of God. The beauty as such is never influenced or affected by transitory affairs and happenings of day-to-day life. Naturally, One as Tagore visualises remains in quietude and beautiful in all serenity and poignancy in this vast universe by overcoming the barriers like birth, death, sorrow happiness etc.

(b) One remains eternally beautiful even under diversities.

(c) One is the strength of all strength, the peace of all peace and the blessing of all blessings.

(d) The idea of One in the world of humankind is that of goodness revealed from different perspectives and expressed in diverse manners.

Tagore also exposes religion in terms of work with which anyone is associated. If the work is not directed towards calmness and peace of mind, the realisation of One through work as worship remains blurred. Therefore, whatever work is enriched and ennobled with forbearance and peace contributes to one's devotion to the religion of One where all constraints are turned into pleasure and all emotional propensities of the heart are adorned with beauty and goodness. The heartland of humankind welcomes One as the All Beautiful who blesses us with the perfect vision of true religion. Let erudition be disseminated everywhere in all sobriety and humility. Let the heart be filled in with the grandeur of One.

That work in joy and creativity is work in worship finds an aura of efflorescence in Tagore's concept of religion. This religion becomes accessible to one and all because it starts in simplicity and unassuming creativity amidst the vastness of the universe and embraces serenity in joy and wonder, mystery and silence, calmness and depth of vision. The boundless spirit of Brahma elevates one in such a creative and aesthetic canvas for the pursuit of religion of all religions proclaiming the prized ascent of man. Work then becomes an incomparable offering of devotion to the All Serene or it symbolically turns the unassuming All Serene effulgent in joy delivered from it or sorrows and sufferings undergone and experienced through it. Work is self-divinised in *Visvakarma,* the God of universal work, where the concept of religion as Tagore succinctly represents finds a depth of devotion in salutation to instruments and appliances symbolically suggesting the embodiment of the All Serene.

The religious concept emanating from work in the vision of *Visvakarma* as Tagore idealises and practises in poignancy adds three components of religion as a radical force of self-illumination. First, let religion represented through work be primarily a humanised efflorescence so that work never becomes a humdrum routine-conscious affair, a mechanical drudgery. Second, let all work directed towards the end-in-view of religion be a fountain of and brought up in the midst of spontaneity. Third, the religion represented in or by work be enriched in profusion and prosperity of joy and freedom. Tagore accentuates the concept of religion as such not because he wants to represent religion by means of work as we generally mean but essentially because he has an incomparable and extraordinary vision of the religion of creativity and critically penetrating into the majestic world of Brahma, the world of enlightenment for the rebirth of man.

Quite apart from other religious thinkers, Tagore also visualises every work as the embodiment of the All Serene. He refashions and re-fabricates religion in course of devotion to work not like a strict disciplinarian or like a hard task master but like a homeless wanderer, a *Baul* or a roving minstrel in eternal quest for the All Beautiful. He, therefore, extends or flashes in every creative fullness of vision with a transcendental force—*Charaiveti*—the march on and on for realisation of true religion. This makes the concept of religion as he unfolds and manifests quite different and distinctive, where all visions of transfer and transcendence that he flashes by means of exercising boundless joy and creativity make a worthy and serene advancement of trans-valuation of values and enrichment of consciousness.

To Tagore, religion is never an independent, separate or different entity isolated from life but it is a symphony that has kinship with everything in life which brings about unity in differences, peace in conflict and harmony in every form of incoherence. It is life which is wedded to the promise and poignancy of building a bridge between different mind-sets. The odyssey of religion as Tagore advocates is one of open mindedness where it muses on the victory of man blessed with deliverance from the so-called religion and ritualism encapsulated in a part of humanity being totally dissociated from and chided by politics, divorced by battles, banished by utilitarianism or neglected by day-to-day happiness of life. It mingled in deep life and sincerity of purpose with all our knowledge and appreciation, sorrow and happiness, loneliness and togetherness enjoying emancipation as it were from the walled city of the mind in diverse disciplines.

Tagore always keeps religion apart from compartmentalisation that more often than not cares for nursling of sectarianism and fundamentalism. Nor does he allow religion to be divorced from age-old rich tradition where the existence of the All Serene enjoys ageless welcome. This he further consolidates with a specific example. Unlike the change of seasons year after year, the rich identity of religion proclaiming the glory of man never undergoes any change. The greatest ideas and ideals of religion enjoy eternal warmth of welcome to anyone who adores Truth, the most invaluable, oldest and greatest component of religion.

Tagore further conceptualises religion with its earnest identity resplendent in the fine component of openness. True religion is almost wide open for anyone anywhere. So it needs no dissemination. Better is it to say that it is beyond dissemination. It is self-disseminating, and as it is so, it needs neither protection nor dissemination either by an individual or by a group or even through so-called centres of religion. This is why building religious institutions from this particular viewpoint is a mockery or vainglory in the names of cultivation and dissemination of religion. This buries all good sense and sensibilities in understanding and appreciating the inner worth of religion and creates or encourages fronts to be in constant guard against the so-called safeguard of religion which turns out as irreligion by giving priorities to vested interests. Indeed, the modern world with all its acme of modernity fails to attract anyone to cast off religiosity in different centres of worship of any or every religion. Meanwhile, in our country as well, one is banished from the invaluable concept of religion that embraces life in discharging honestly and sincerely different types of solemn activities like duties and responsibilities towards the guests, the members of the family far or near, the community, the society, the nation and the world at large besides being justified to the self.

Tagore intensifies religion as a positive mark of humanism where the mind of man plays a very significant role in unison of boundless joy with a very balanced and controlled mode of living. He, therefore, allows no hypocrisy or dubious ambiguity. Instead, he encourages cultivation of spontaneity and simplicity as natural outcome of religion. This religion of India as he time and again highlights is never interested in virtue and vice as such and in the interest of advancement of contentment accelerates the mind towards the qualities of ascent and excellence.

The three essential components of religion as Tagore emphasises in terms of the above are happiness, contentment and control of the mind. But for understanding and appreciating true religion he warns that these cannot be fruitful unless all these components are practised in absolute fusion. Again, in order to avert and eliminate subjectivity as best as possible and make religion the religion of man, all these components all the time necessitate crystallisation. Tagore's own elucidation on this point clarifies the idea better—what he wants to justify is to prepare everyone to be a true exponent of religion by rising up to the most prized vision of manhood so that everyone is continually striving to be awakened, effulged, established and, above all, to be simple and amiable. The mind should serve as the mirror of joy ineffable. Let the mind remain calm and serene even under trying circumstances. Let the pool, as it were, of the mind enjoy undisturbed poignancy of happiness, contentment and control.

In elucidating the true concept of religion, Tagore refers to the important end-in-view as delineated in the Upanishad: *Santosang hridi sangsthaya sukharthi sangyato bhavet.* Therefore, to be restrained in tone and temperament as a man of true contentment is the genuine way of highlighting true religion. This serves three-fold purpose. First, there is absolute sacrifice of egoism. Second, the mind enjoys free discipline in sheer joy and simplicity. Third, religion becomes a master of our very own—an endearing zenith of excellence and ascent of man. How to make a worthwhile synchronisation between religion and humanism? What are the essential components of religion through which it becomes an inseparable and living reality to mankind? Quite apart from other religious thinkers and humanists, Tagore emphasises on the fact that true religion is interested not in virtue or vice and the manifold application of either of the two from the narrow sense of culture of virtue or vice as such unrelated to humane sensibilities. He distinctly delves deep into the core of humanism and religion not separately but in unison between the two. The consequence is thrilling and living, practical and just. He clearly defines religion as the union of the mind with its boundless joyous being and, therefore, it becomes an endless quest for joy.

With the conceptual framework of religion as the quest for joy, Tagore makes a definite and signal departure from stereotyped concepts of prayer and devotion as marks of religion. He makes an introspective analysis of religion from the perspective of prayer with three specific points of view. First, all religion and, therefore, all prayer should be directed towards Truth. Truth makes religion more comprehensive and allied to humanity. It shines in the lustre of seeing oneself both within and outside with all seriousness of purpose. Second, all religion must be directed towards natural efflorescence which is, as it were, the halo of religion. Third, religion must be a quest for the nectar of humanity in fusion with the All Serene.

Tagore elucidates the genesis of prayer as an exponent of religion exquisitely. How should one be devoted to prayer? The answer he suggests is remarkable. Every endeavour on our part at prayer in its very beginning should be to exactly and appropriately come to know what we specifically pray for, and why. Unless this initial objective is taken for serious consideration, the striving for prayer as a religious exercise becomes ambiguous and, of course, erroneous. The end-in-view of religion also remains inoperative and attainment of success in prayer becomes blurred. On the other hand, a positive step in this direction to primarily specify our ends-in-view of prayer makes success distinct and certain.

Moreover, with such a comprehensive quest for religion by means of prayer, a certain sense of altruism embracing the entire human race irrespective of colour and clime develops within oneself with all endearing spontaneity. This great aspiration for awakening of altruistic humanism is the keynote of prayer as a mark of true religion.

With prayer as the focal point of religion, Tagore adorns religion with the world of aesthetics. In fact, he visualises and concentrates on religion not as a matter of ritualistic exercise either in the form of renunciation or in that of isolation from diverse attachments but essentially a devotion to the quest for joy. He categorically asserts that true religion is in essence the religion of joy and attachment to everything in and around us, which allows and enriches us to have the eternal pleasure of the taste of freedom. His philosophy of religion, therefore, makes ample room for devotion to joy and freedom which encompass the unending beauty of religion. As he very poignantly asserts in one of the poems of *Naivedya,*

Vairagyasadhane mukti se amar nay
Asankhya vandhan majhe mahanandamay
Labhiva muktir swad

To have emancipation by means of renunciation is alien to me,

In the trammels of innumerable constraints would I taste emancipation full of great joy.

[Translated by me]

What type of joy does Tagore endear in his philosophy of religion? What are the principal characteristics of the joy that he untiringly seeks? A probing approach to such questions for appropriate answers would allow one to encounter the following:

(a) Tagore visualises religion as the exponent of joy assuring one to be true to oneself. This also indicates the fact that the religion one should cater to and nourish is one of spontaneity of one's very being. *Anandadhara vahichhe bhuvane*—the spring of joy is flowing in the world, as Tagore characteristically asserts, and that fountain of joy is the true identity of religion.

(b) Whatever joy one receives out of purity and poignancy, devotion and perseverance in one's sustained endeavour becomes the hallmark of religion as it truly represents the truth and beauty of joy.

(c) An adventure into the world of joy, indeed, is a challenge to every form of dissipation and distraction from which one continually suffers in a mess of narrowness and misappropriation of the true concept of religion. Such an adventure is primarily geared towards ascent and excellence, brilliance and depth of vision.

(d) Tagore emphasises on joy as a very important component of religion essentially because it does not allow religion to be complex and crude, rigid and dogmatic. On the other hand, such religion well nourished and vitalised in joy broadens the vision of religious askance and fullness.

(e) Tagore's philosophy of religion in communion with joy also ensures transparency, judiciousness, simplicity and clarity. He does not allow religion to be a victim of utter anti-religion but religion-friendly in the sense that religion becomes one's very own rather than mere rituals in rugged and ruptured exercise of mechanical deprivation of joy.

(f) The religion of joy derived from simplicity makes ample room for exercise of freedom whereby religion becomes a process of self-enquiry, self-realisation, self-analysis and self-evaluation. This type of religion which has its deep roots in joy makes it more adaptable to the changing needs and conditions of the mind and the heart. This has two-fold advantage: first, such religion bred and illumined in joy paves a newer dimension of religion par excellence, and second, such religion becomes an object of perennial quest within oneself for Truth, Goodness and Beauty which unendingly contribute towards enrichment and fullness of man.

The concept of joy that Tagore assimilates in his concept of religion makes the latter more adorable and abiding than simply toying with its matter-of-factness as we very often witness. He makes newer inroads of the vision par excellence which permeates in the aura of efflorescence essentially mystic and, therefore, a progressive approach to the sensible and serene beyonding of consciousness. Moreover, he makes an ardent approach to his intimate relationship with the All Serene where the mystic vision finds fullness in cadence and catholicity. As he significantly muses:

Thus it is that thy joy in me is so full.
Thus it is that thou hast come down to me.
O thou lord of all heavens, where would
be thy love if I were I not?

Thou hast taken me as thy partner of
all this wealth. In my heart is the endless play
of thy delight. In my life thy will is ever taking
shape.
And for this, thou who art the King of kings
Hast decked thyself in beauty to captivate my heart.
And for this thy love loses itself in the love of thy
lover,
and there art thou seen in the perfect union of two.

—Rabindranath Tagore:*Gitanjali,* Macmillan India Limited, New Delhi, Macmillan Pocket Tagore Edition, 1983, No. LVI, p. 37.

For Tagore, religion becomes an entry point of joy and vice versa, where love becomes the guiding spirit of religion. It is love and love in all its serenity which crystallises the concept of religion in tune with the best of humility in oneself shared and disseminated in mystic grandeur.

Tagore expands the horizon of love not merely in tune with the mystic beyonding but also in action and dedication where it becomes akin to humanism. To him, littleness is alien to man as the latter stands for religion embodied, enhanced, effulged and crystallised. He feels the inner urge of the spirit of man undaunted, ever victorious, ever respondent to the All True that beckons within every human being. He explores and re-fabricates the essentials of humanism which in its purity and perfection hails and honours religion pertaining to devotion and dedication through action and ardent contemplation.

Tagore accelerates the spirit of religion towards spiritualism where man finds the strength that eliminates all narrowness of mind and partisan approach to any involvement. He directs and decorates religion with that cadence and grandeur of spirituality where ascent and excellence become the hallmark of human endeavour. As a matter of fact, his concept of religion so adroitly nursed in spiritual vision makes the former accessible and abiding to every individual earnestly thriving for excellence in individuality. Hence, creativity serves as the exponent of religion in right practice, right progress, right expression, right exercise and right status of the unity of the mind and the heart.

That spirituality exercised in and through religion makes religion more adorable and enlivening than merely undergoing rites and rituals paves newer avenues of advancement of creativity. Religion thus becomes more dynamic in the process of acceleration of noble thoughts and visions for man. The religion that fosters spirituality forsakes littleness and welcomes greatness where the little 'I' is blessed with the great 'We' in order to be in fusion with the All Serene endlessly beckoning for ascent and excellence.

Tagore makes religion a perfect component of the essence of spirituality so that religiousness rather than religiosity becomes the benchmark of human progress. He upholds spirituality not merely as another feat of religion or an exercise towards another direction but especially for crystallisation of the self to be in perfect union with the Supreme Self. This may ostensibly seem abstract and bizarre but Tagore makes a simplistic approach which has its rooms and roots deeply in human nature. That man is spiritual and, therefore, devotes and adores religion not by an externally imposed force unassumingly by an internal, intrinsic, creative and spontaneous natural force is the true concept of religion which nurtures spirituality within itself and voiced forth by man in his very being and beyonding of consciousness. Tagore thus widens the horizon of religion from the qualitative paradigm of human evolution in fostering spirituality when all littleness is purified in terms of vastness and the finite finds fullness in the infinite and endless.

The excellence of religion that Tagore seeks in all contemplations and actions is that of spirituality and the excellence of spirituality proves man as the true representative of the All Serene. He recalls the great saying of the Upanishad characterising man as *amritasya putrah,* the sons of the Immortal Deathless and highlights the eternal victory of man in the victory of spirituality which is the essence of religion. He, therefore, maintains and emphasises on better cultivation of the religion of man so that the littleness emanating from the narrower bonds or sects of irreligion becomes purified and crystallised in perfect and serene exercise of spirituality.

As an incomparable exponent of religion, Tagore draws our attention to the simpler and nobler exposition of religion as reflected in nature and natural objects. He motivates our attention to whatever appears to us as meaningless, purposeless, abstract and useless and stimulates us to make a radical and revolutionary approach to ward off all superstitions and conjectures associated with the mystery of nature. He simply tells us to be natural with nature and humane with human beings, emotions and sensibilities. These have a four-fold advantage. The first and the foremost one is that we associate ourselves to be genuine partners with wonder and askance, vision and vastness, nobility and greatness.

Second, we satisfy our infinite thirst for knowing the unknown and feeling the intrinsic spirit of the endless and the infinite. Third, we nourish the spirit of self-realisation in the undeterred and unending domain of freedom and silence. Fourth, we continually make an earnest endeavour to the partners of endless joy wherefrom the different elements and objects of nature find their manifestations. While wonder widens the horizon of religion, it also welcomes awe and serenity. This is why Tagore embraces nature and natural objects not only as our very own but also as our very existence, our essence, our enviable eternal strength which in untiring and natural exercise from our ends turns out to be a luminous and radiant image of spirituality. He refers to this type of quest for religion as the inhaling and exhaling of religion in the midst of nature.

The spirit of the endless and the infinite writ large in nature brings forth religion in its most serene and vibrant form. Tagore appreciates this spirit not as a mere natural phenomenon but as the life force that teaches one how to be in perfect fusion with the Supreme Being. He exalts upon this with a buoyant spirit of his unending indebtedness to nature where silence, sunrise, gloom and slumber find a language of unfathomable poignancy. This, then, is religion bred and nourished in the womb of spirituality as Tagore characterises in disseminating the language of inward spiritual vision:

> The morning sea of silence broke into ripples of bird songs; and the flowers were all merry by the roadside; and the wealth of gold was scattered through the rift of the clouds while we busily went on our way and paid no heed.

We sang no glad songs nor played; we went not to the village for barter; we spoke not a word nor smiled; we lingered not on the way. We quickened our pace more and more as the time sped by.

The sun rose to the mid sky and doves cooed in the shade. Withered leaves danced and whirled in the hot air of noon. The shepherd boy drowsed and dreamed in the shadow of the banyan tree, and I laid myself down by the water and stretched my tired limbs on the grass.

My companions laughed at me in scorn; they held their heads high and hurried on; they never looked back nor rested; they vanished in the distant blue haze. They crossed many meadows and hills, and passed through strange, far-away countries. All honour to you, heroic host of the interminable path! Mockery and reproach pricked me to rise, but found no response in me. I gave myself up for lost in the depth of a glad humiliation–in the shadow of a dim light.

The repose of the sun-embroidered green gloom slowly spread over my heart. I forgot for what I had travelled, and I surrendered my mind without struggle to the maze of shadows and songs.

At last, when I woke from my slumber and opened my eyes, I saw thee standing by me, flooding my sleep with thy smile. How I had

feared that the path was long and wearisome,
and the struggle to reach thee was hard!

—*Ibid.*, pp. 29-30.

A certain sense of religion best crystallised in spirituality as Tagore fathoms in his vision of the All Serene goes a long way in unveiling the nuances of religion that stand for man, the incomparable exponent of the All Serene in everyone, everything and within himself. With all harrowing of delusion and desolation, man's eternal quest for unison with the Innermost One becomes a vibrant reality with the awakening of all awakenings from the slumber of passion and emotional destabilisation. The search for Atman or the self in the true identity of oneself goes on while the spirit in one endorses self-purification by means of self-askance and self-enquiry. Hence, there is the sheer importance of nourishing the spirit of self-realisation in the unhindered and boundless sky of freedom and silence leading to the religion of the soul which, indeed, is the soul of religion.

Admittedly, Tagore makes the world of religion infinite in the sense that true religion always makes room for embracing freedom and silence not as isolated entities but as a unified whole enabling one to make a ceaseless quest for the All Serene in one's own fashion of nursling the spirit of the depth of silence. That silence becomes the All Serene in the unruffled atmosphere of freedom awaits an intimate and cordial relationship with Nature where the latter becomes an adorable voice of the infinite spirit within which extends the horizon of religion in the essence of spirituality. As soon as one feels and becomes one with Nature, the spirit within one finds the vision of excellence and ascent which best defines and represents religion in the crystallised vision of spirituality. The finer sensibilities within oneself permeate in their essence the language of the soul which is the language of true religion in the revered spirit of the sublime. Tagore's own experimentation in this regard elucidates the point best in the muse as follows:

> I have had my invitation to this world's festival, and thus my life has been blessed. My eyes have seen and my ears have heard.
>
> It was my part at this feast to play upon my instrument, and I have done all I could.
>
> Now, I ask, has the time come at last when I may go in and see thy face and offer thee my silent salutation?

—*Ibid.*, p. 10.

A mystic journey towards making an encounter with the All Serene leaves apart all vicissitudes and ignorance and upholds the truth of religion that knows no bondage or narrowness. As a matter of fact, Tagore makes religion more comprehensive in welcoming us into the world of infinite beauty and grandeur where we breathe an air of cohesion and compromise of whatever is best in every religion either in letter or in observance. He instils a new spirit of religion in all purity and intensity of vision so that the beckoning of fullness is never allowed to be lost in the maize of miasma or confusion.

Tagore exalts and heightens the spirit of religion by infusing the spirit of mysticism which breathes an air of adoration and serenity, fulfilment and magnanimity. He invites the Holy Grail of human consciousness where religion becomes a boon and guiding spirit of human emotions and sensibilities crystallised and communicated to the Man of the Heart—*maner manush*—as he cordially invites the All Serene.

Being attuned to the serene depth of mystic vision as above, Tagore unveils the spirit of religion in the spirit of the masses in the entire human society where the spirit makes a reawakening of the human soul which is the right representative of the Divine Soul. He felicitates the poor and the ignorant, the simple and austere spirit of the peasants and the working classes where he re-instils the spirit of religion in the practical poignancy of work as worship. He pays his humble reverence to the tillers of the land, the weavers of the dark hovels, the blacksmith of the gloomy dens and the artisans of the dilapidated thatches with the same sense of respectability and adoration as one pays homage to the gods and the goddesses or the prophets and the parsons. He even goes a step further in alienating oneself from reformations and dissemination of religious teachings as such by treading on the lone but living path of religion where religion becomes the voice of the man ever victorious in the fulfilment of the visions of Truth, Beauty and Goodness.

An incomparable and unparalleled forerunner of religion as it should truly represent man and society, Tagore conceptualises religion as the true identity of man as 'men' and vice versa in relation to the All Serene. He makes an unending quest for a religion of religions where man harbours on a new lotus-land of grace and dignity of the self embodying and translating the spirit of the Supreme Self. This is not all. As a mystic visionary par excellence, he accentuates the spirit of religion towards a spirit of advancement of human values and sensibilities always looking for the glory of the unknown in course of tireless strivings stretching arms towards fullness.

Do we respond?

2

Religion and Functions and Festivals: Tagorean Quest

Religion is what one wholeheartedly embodies within oneself in contemplation and action. It is devotion and dedication to disciplined involvements well backed and nursed by joy, freedom and creativity in every contemplation and action as Rabindranath Tagore elaborates the horizon of true religion in terms of mankind, where spontaneity and self-enquiry are the endless guiding spirit of human development.

Quite apposite to human developments and sensibilities, Tagore places the altar of religion of the heartland of human wills and aspirations. He identifies it as a positive approach to man's endless strivings for union with the All Serene who lives in and around in Nature and natural surroundings. He enshrines it as a *vrata,* an askesis, for union with the Lord of askesis—*Vratapati.* He, therefore, visualises the Lord of askesis from daily happenings of life with observance of different functions and festivals which are nothing but translating components of one's quest for true religion. This has its three-fold factor contributing to a gradual and disciplined approach to knowing, feeling and sticking to what religion truly stands for man's onward march for true humanism in relation to divinity and vice versa. The first factor contributing to such ends-in-view of religion is a spontaneous and careful approach to Truth to eliminate all narrowness and apathy, superstition and segregation for emancipation. Second, a course of simplicity and generosity clubbed with humility and patience is justified in representing religion of the highest order of honouring man as the embodiment of the All Serene. Third, a steady and silent march for self-knowledge, self-realisation and self-surrender should always highlight the glory of the All Serene where religion teaches the lesson of how to transform and transcend oneself to a cipher.

The functions and festivals of Santiniketan and Sriniketan that bear and represent Tagore's faith in the ideas and ideals of religion in the light of the above may be itemised and identified in terms of dates of observances as follows:

Name of the Function / Festival	*Month / Date(s)*
Navavarsa and Rabindra-Janmotsava	April 14
Dharmacakra Pravartana	July
Varsamangal & vriksharopana	July-August
Rabindra-Smaran	August 8-9
Silpotsava	September 17
Saradotsava	September
Paus Utsava	December 21-24
Christotsava	December 25
Maharshi Smarana	January 20
Sriniketan Utsava	February 6-8
Gandhi Punyaha	March 10
Vasantotsava	March
Varsa-ses	April

Admittedly, the purpose behind the observance of each function and festival at Visva-Bharati is to practise the religion of how to endear and associate oneself in complete compliances with peace, harmony, vastness, pleasure and profusion of Nature which ennoble and enrich the best of divinity in the best spirit of ascent and excellence of humanism. In fact, Tagore brings forth and revitalises a new concept of religion where the image of man stands out in shining brilliance professed and blessed in spiritual marvels.

It is interesting to note in this connection how, in spite of being born and brought up in a Brahma family, Tagore aims at a cosmological approach to religion where he brings to the fore the spirit of human ascent and excellence merged in the spirit of unison with the All Serene. This is why he welcomes every religion in his Visva-Bharati—*Yatra visvam bhavatyekanidam*—where the world makes its home in a single nest, nurturing and cultivating the abiding and stimulating spirit of every religion contributing to the march of finer human sensibilities and higher visions of life. Thus while the spirit of Buddhism finds manifestation in the observance of *Dharmacakra Pravartana* or in highlighting the spirit of *Karuna* in the dramatic presentations of *Chandalika* or *Chitrangada* and others in which he himself takes parts and, more often than not, writes scripts of short plays meant for children in particular, he strives to infuse the spirit of true religion where the functional aspects of the essence of religion find a new language of vision and depth.

Apart from the fact that religion is the quest for inwardness of vision for better self-realisation, Tagore directs our attention towards the nobler aspects of religion embracing grace and depth, grandeur and perseverance.

In fact, his main concern for infusing the spirit of religion amongst children in his own institutions at Visva-Bharati is to make them aware of these finer components of religion not by rigorously following some rules and regulations of religious laws and principles, rites and rituals, but by introducing a spontaneous and free atmosphere of exercise of religion through active participation in functions and festivals highlighting all the finer components of religion in a joyous spirit of exercise.

Tagore also directs our attention to the fact that everyone aspires after self-consciousness. This urge for self-efflorescence by means of self-involvement haunts everyone to realise and assess his role as an individual in terms of Truth which leads to his emancipation. As such, Tagore encourages everyone to be devoted to duties and responsibilities towards the society in order to be hallowed with the spirit of unfolding himself for the goodness of others and this is what he means by the religion of Truth, the religion of *apavrinu*—the religion of emancipation of the self.

With the religion of the emancipation of the self as above, Tagore clarifies the vision of participation in different functions and festivals which enable everyone to be truly civilised. In fact, he categorically explains the real meaning of the term 'civilisation' from the perspective of true religion as follows:

> The true meaning of the word civilisation is to have oneself amidst a congregation, to understand oneself in the midst of all. The root meaning of the word 'meeting' is that where there is lustre, there is light. This means that

> he light of a man's efflorescence is not within his own self, but in union with all. Where there is paucity of this theory of unison, the truth of mankind is wrapped up there to that very extent. For this very reason man is all the time speaking to his own self—*'apavrinu'*, unfold, unfold the covering of thy own self, manifest thyself with the truth of all and thee. Therein lies the efflorescence, thy emancipation.
>
> —Rabindranath Tagore: "Visva-Bharati", *Rabindra-Rachanavali,* Government of West Bengal, Calcutta, 1992, Vol. XIV, P. 512.
>
> [Translated by me]

The spirit of unfolding oneself for the greater interest of others anywhere in order to manifest good sense and sensibilities is what Tagore identifies as the true spirit of religion. It is this spirit which should be exercised in different functions and festivals which, indeed, are the multi-dimensional avenues of what one wants to practise for the religious efflorescence of Truth, Beauty and Goodness.

The genesis of functions and festivals as Tagore reveals in his different statements on how to identify and translate them in pursuit of strength and, therefore, of religion is itself a glorification of the indomitable spirit of man , the embodiment of the All Serene. Every function and festival as he serenely visualises is a ceremony of this strength of the mind and the heart fulfilling the missions of great sacrifice and earnest involvements which represent the true image of the All Serene.

How to appreciate the vision of the All Serene in the light of functions and festivals? What for are functions and festivals so far as realisation of the Eternal Spirit is concerned? Tagore's own elucidation on these queries deserves our attention:

> What ceremony do we observe today? It is the ceremony of strength. What an astonishing strength is being revealed amidst man in a surprising manner! Overcoming all his paltry needs, to what an ascent man stands apart! Amid what an unending invincible journey the wise being is treading on! To what an untiring and unattainable endeavour has a worker made a fearless entry! Commemorating the glory of that immeasurable strength which has been revealed in the erudition, love and action of man, we would observe that ceremony today. Not as individuals but as man we would identify this oneness of us today.
>
> —*Ibid.,* p. 614.
>
> [Translated by me]

With the ceremony of strength representing the ceremony of religion, Tagore unfolds a new dimension of religion which sets apart rites and rituals and ennobles the vision of Truth, Beauty and Goodness. At the same time, he directs our attention towards realisation of the diverse forces of the universe leading to an intrinsic harmony and fulfilling the end-in-view of realisation of the finite and the infinite in love. He embraces a conflict of the opposites considering these as components of harmony in lieu of chaos. As a true seeker of religion, one cannot but welcome the conflicts of the opposing forces of the universe which bring forth 'the mystery of all mysteries' as the characteristic vision of One. Therefore, the functions and festivals related to endearing of the opposites of this universe is religion par excellence where the evolution of human sensibilities finds a fitting avenue of efflorescence. Tagore's own characteristic deliberation in this connection deserves a re-thinking in right earnest:

> The real is the infinite, and it is only *maya,* the unreality, which causes the appearance of the finite. But the word *maya* is a mere name, it is no explanation. It is merely saying that with truth there is this appearance which is the opposite of truth; but how they come to exist at one and the same time is incomprehensible.
>
> We have what we call in Sanskrit *dvandva,* a series of opposites in creation; such as, the positive pole and the negative, the centripetal force and the centrifugal, attraction and repulsion. These are also mere names, they are no explanations. They are only different ways of asserting that the world in its essence is a reconciliation of pairs of opposing forces. These forces, like the left and the right hands of the creator, are acting in absolute harmony, yet acting from opposite directions.
>
> There is a bond of harmony between our two eyes, which makes them all in unison. Likewise there is an unbreakable continuity of relation in the physical world between heat and cold, light and darkness, motion and rest, as between the bass and the treble notes of a

piano. This is why these opposites do not bring confusion in the universe, but harmony. If creation were but a chaos, we should have to imagine the two opposing principles as trying to get the better of each other. But the universe is not under martial law, arbitrary and provisional. Here we find no force which can run amok, or go on indefinitely in the wild road, like an exiled outlaw, breaking all harmony with its surroundings; each force, on the contrary, has to come back in a curved line to its equilibrium. Waves rise, each in its individual height in a seeming attitude of unrelenting competition, but only up to a certain point, and thus we know of the great repose of the sea to which they must all return in rhythm which is marvellously beautiful.

In fact, these undulations and vibrations, these risings and fallings, are not due to the erratic contortions of disparate bodies; they are a rhythmic dance. Rhythm can never be born of the haphazard struggle of combat. Its underlying principle must be unity, not opposition.

This principle of unity is the mystery of all mysteries. The existence of a duality at once raises a question in our minds, and we seek its solution in the One. When at last we find a relation between these two, and thereby see them as one in essence, we feel that we have come to the truth. And then we give utterance to this most startling of all paradoxes, that the

> One appears as many, that the appearance is the opposite of truth and yet it is inseparably related to it.
>
> -Rabindranath Tagore: "Realisation of Love", *Sadhana,* Macmillan India Limited, New Delhi, Macmillam Pocket Tagore Edition, 1979, pp. 79-81.

The quest for harmony in conflict revealed in the mystery of the universe as Tagore seeks through the principle of unity—'the mystery of all mysteries'—embraces Nature as the most potent force where the search for rhythm awaits a nursling of the festivals and the functions which bring forth the joyous spirit and freedom of the universe in natural surroundings a new habitation and name amidst humans. This is what he christens as the religion of Nature—the religion that unfolds Truth, Beauty and Goodness.

Admittedly, the significance of functions and festivals from the standpoint of religion as Tagore manifests in his philosophy of religion may be spelt out from the following dimensions:

(i) Aesthetic vision
(ii) Mystic vision
(iii) Spiritual vision

With all functions and festivals related to the invocation of Nature and seasonal changes, Tagore wants to highlight the spirit of aesthetics in the exercise of creativity, joy, freedom and spontaneity. All these components contribute to crystallisation of religious sensibilities where Truth emerges in an aura of ephemeral delight, Beauty becomes buoyant in thrilling exercise of joy and creativity, and Goodness spreads the ardent and serene veil of sobriety and calmness where peace reigns supreme.

As regards mystic vision, Tagore expands the horizon of human consciousness and encourages all attempts to grasp the essence of whatever heightens the human mind towards the endless exercise of devotion to best thoughts, best emotions, best sensibilities and best depth of vision. This is why he introduces different functions and festivals related to Nature and her abundant sombre rhythm and grandeur. He also inspires to enjoy the warmth of Nature by means of functions and festivals to be attuned to the infinite spirit which broadens the human mind to be closely associated with the vastness as revealed in the open sky, the sun, the moon, the stars and the milky way—all embracing eternal mystery and wonder.

Admittedly, Tagore's mystic vision as delineated in observance of functions and festivals welcomes an unprecedented stamp of sincerity and depth of inward vision of the human mind where the beckoning of the light eternal are always rewarded with a perfume of promise and fullness. The Poet's own adoration of the festival of light finds a mystic efflorescence in full glory and splendour in his own muse as follows:

> Light, my light, the world-filling light, the eye-kissing light, heart-sweetening light!
>
> Ah, the light dances, my darling, at the centre of my life; the light strikes, my darling, the chords of my love; the sky opens, the wind runs wild, laughter passes over the earth.

> The butterflies spread their sails on the sea of light. Lilies and jasmines surge up on the crest of the waves of light.
>
> The light is shattered into gold on every cloud, my darling, and it scatters gems in profusion.
>
> Mirth spreads from leaf to leaf, my darling, and gladness without measure. The heaven's river has drowned its banks and the flood of joy is abroad.
>
> —Rabindranath Tagore: *Gitanjali*, Macmillan India Limited, New Delhi, Macmillan Pocket Tagore Edition, 1983, No. LVII, pp. 37-38.

The world of mystic beauty and endlessness as Tagore highlights in functions and festivals has its rhythmic charm which enchants the mind and prepares the soul to mingle in the festival of light and joy in all askance and wonder. This mystic world as existent in the vastness of Nature also ensures the infinite strength for mankind to be born anew by eliminating all narrowness and selfish trivialities in order to be in fusion with the boundless beauty and grandeur of the universe to embody the prized greatness of personality. In fact, he unfolds an incomparable world of mystic awareness in idealising the vibrant Nature through functions and festivals in order to negotiate the nagging problems of the self imprisoned in the world-force that aggravates tension and pollutes the mind with puerile thoughts and passive visions of crudity and callousness.

In analysing the problem of self, Tagore delves deep into the mystic inwardness of the individual where the efflorescence of individuality depends on how to welcome and appreciate life like the river of a poem representing newness and inner freedom of harmony exercised amidst functions and festivals to learn the lesson of humility and love. The lesson of mystic self-surrender enhancing pride of personality is what he earnestly sensitises in his quest for the true meaning of our self awaiting 'revelation of the Infinite':

> It is for our self to know that it must be born anew every moment of its life. It must break through all illusions that encase it in their crust to make it appear old, burdening it with death.
>
> For life is immortal youthfulness, and it hates age that tries to clog its movements—age that belongs not to life in truth, but follows it as the shadow follows the lamp.
>
> Our life, like a river, strikes its banks not to find itself closed in by them, but to realise anew every moment that it has its unending opening towards the sea. It is as a poem that strikes its metre at every step not to be silenced by its rigid regulations, but to give expression every moment to the inner freedom of its harmony.
>
> The boundary walls of our individuality thrust us back within our limits, on the one hand, and thus lead us, on the other, to the unlimited. Only when we try to make these

limits infinite are we launched into an impossible contradiction and court miserable failure.

This is the cause which leads to the great revolutions in human history. Whenever the part, spurning the whole, tries to run a separate course of its own, the great pull of the all gives it a violent wrench, stops it suddenly, and brings it to the dust. Whenever the individual tries to damn the ever-flowing current of the world-force and imprison it within the area of his particular use, it brings on disaster. However powerful a king may be, he cannot raise his standard of rebellion against the infinite source of strength, which is unity, and yet remain powerful.

It has been said, *By unrighteousness men prosper, gain what they desire, and triumph over their enemies, but at the end they are cut off at the root and suffer extinction.*[1] Our roots must go deep down into the universal if we could attain the greatness of personality.

It is the end ot our self to seek that union. It must bend its head low in love and meekness and take its stand where great and small all meet. It has to gain by its loss and rise by its surrender. His games would be a horror to the child if he could not come back to his mother, and our pride of personality will be a curse to us if we cannot give it up in love. We must know that it is only the revelation of the Infinite

> which is endlessly new and eternally beautiful in us and gives the only meaning to our self.
>
> —Rabindranath Tagore: "The Problem of Self", *Sadhana,* Macmillan India Limited, New Delhi, Macmillan Pocket Tagore Edition, 1983, pp. 74-75.

The revelation of the Infinite as Tagore seeks in his mystic vision of the self signals an altogether new dimension of religion where the self is enriched in vastness and encompassed in the warmth of love and humility, righteousness and dedication. As a spiritual connoisseur par excellence, he extends the inwardness of religion towards a distinct depth of efflorescence and aroma of poignancy, and this he continually experiments through functions and festivals. Every function and festival thus becomes the fountain of freedom—freedom from all littleness and an insignificantly selfish approach to growth and development of personality.

Tagore explores the world of spirituality in the festival of ceremonies which includes the celebration of Truth in joyousness and endlessness. He unfolds Truth as the infinite spirit of the All Serene and this can be translated in life in the realisation of reality of joy. He visualises the All Serene not merely in accepting the fact that the spiritual vision of the latter is encompassed in the concept of His being beyond language and mind but in the natural realisation that He radiates in light, enlivens us in the exercise of joy and reveals in the eternal effulgence of light and sound. Even then, the celebration of spirituality awaits a more thrilling exercise of inhaling and exhaling the spirit of Nature which gloriously delights us in unfolding with boundless vision the All Serene in all catholicity and magnanimity of everlasting beauty and joy.

With the all-embracing vision of spirituality as above, Tagore embraces religion with that depth of spirituality where joy becomes the breath and life of the human spirit always cultivating in diverse functions and festivals the multi-dimensional wonders of Nature awaiting the unison of the best thoughts and intentions to be nursed by humankind. As a matter of fact, he invites us to glorify the ostensibly insignificant components of Nature in the light of the spirit of beauty and grandeur, joy and wonder so that the lesson of spirituality as an ascending and crystallised vision of religion may find a fitting expression in worthwhile functions and festivals.

In an address in1313 B.S., Tagore exquisitely elucidates the concept of spirituality as a chiselled expression of exercise of the religion of light and joy manifested in the most trivial components of Nature like dust and grass. He advises us not to ignore or belittle dust as dust, grass as grass but adore and glorify these as the revelation of joy of the All Joyous. He also advises us to be lively partners of joy as the spirit of the All Joyous actually finds its passage of entry amidst us as messengers of a new awakening of the emergence of religion that fosters spirituality in the heartland of everyone everywhere.

To launch a more intensive exercise of the lesson of spirituality as a heightened vision of religion, Tagore inspires the devotion of transmission and transfusion where one can equip oneself with the most desirable spiritual ability to come out of the day-to-day hub of activities and listen in silence to the spirit of the music inherent in all activities through the spiritual ears. This, if exercised with all sincerity of purpose in course of involvement in functions and festivals, rewards us in four ways:

(a) The weal and woe, the agonies and anxieties, the hopes and frustrations in every nook and corner of human habitation find an endearing affinity to the heart of each individual, where the spiritual vision of joy is revealed in the crystallised religion of knowing the joy of the Brahma, the joy that abounds in every atom of the universe.

(b) The worries of the self aggravated by littleness and tempted by phenomenal glories or triumphs are released by purity of joy and catholicity of thoughts.

(c) There is always an unending beckoning for learning the lesson of fearlessness because such an abiding devotion to spirituality in submitting oneself to the grandeur of silent and serene darkness amidst Nature is actually a devotion to learning a higher lesson of religion that celebrates the ceremony of affluence of blessings showered by the All Serene everywhere.

(d) A sense of mutual cooperation and harmony in quest of spirituality adds to the new dimension of religion of man for which Tagore makes newer inroads to spiritual awareness.

Tagore makes religion more sensible and practicable through introduction and dissemination of functions and festivals. The different functions and festivals observed throughout the year at Visva-Bharati encompass a practical approach to religion which interprets in all true perspectives the realisation of life from diverse perspectives. Religion in its true essence must, as he earnestly believes, conform to the relation of the individual to the universe. For this purpose he emphasises on realisation of religion by means of the exercise of the spirit of comprehension—the spirit of one's very being in perfect manifestation of love. This is why he recalls the spirit of the Upanishads to embrace all in order to be in unison with the All Serene. This lesson to learn how to embrace all necessitates the habitual exercise by an individual through involvements in different functions and festivals which actually represent the spirit of the religion of realisation of relationship between the spirit within and that of the universe. As Tagore characteristically asserts:

> Man can destroy and plunder, earn and accumulate, invent and discover, but he is great because his soul comprehends all. It is dire destruction for him when he envelopes soul in a dead shell of callous habits, and when a blind fury of works whirls round him like an eddying dust storm, shutting out the horizon. That indeed kills the spirit of his being, which is the spirit of comprehension. Essentially man is not a slave either of himself or of the world; but he is a lover. His freedom and fulfilment is in love, which is another name for perfect comprehension. By this power of comprehension, this permeation of his being, he is united with the all-pervading Spirit, who is also the breath of his soul. Where a man tries to raise himself to eminence by pursuing and

jostling all others, to achieve a distinction by which he prides himself to be more than everybody else, there he is alienated from that Spirit. This is why the Upanishads describe those who have attained the goal of human life as '*peaceful*'[2] and as '*at-one-with-God*'[3], meaning that they are in perfect harmony with man and nature, and therefore in undisturbed union with God.

We have a glimpse of the same truth in the teachings of Jesus when he says, 'It is easier for a camel to pass through the eye of a needle than a rich man to enter the kingdom of Heaven'—which implies that whatever we treasure for ourselves separates us from others; our possessions are our limitations. He who is bent upon accumulating riches is unable, with his ego continually bulging, to pass through the gates of comprehension of the spiritual world, which is the world of perfect harmony; he is shut up within the narrow walls of his limited acquisitions.

Hence, the spirit of the Upanishads is: In order to find Him you must embrace all.

—*Ibid.,* pp. 13-14.

Tagore's vision of religious and spiritual culture as manifested in devotion to functions and festivals at Visva-Bharati embodies eclectic and evolutionary spirit of joy and freedom, creativity and spontaneity, discipline and punctuality, righteousness and serenity. The early morning *vaitalik,* the songs of prayer, the solemn congregation, the chanting of the Vedic hymns, the singing of songs related to man and the universe at large keeping Nature and the surroundings in harmonious relationship with the grateful image of man being continually caressed and blessed by the former—all indicate a sense of the great spirit of love and comprehension in which man is in perfect unison with the All Serene. The daily programmes of functions and festivals become a living spirit of the endless pursuit of Beauty, Truth and Goodness, and are never a dull, mechanical drudgery symbolising ritualism.

Indeed, all functions and festivals observed at Visva-Bharati have this inner spirit of joy and freedom which enlivens the soul to be active and resourceful in making an untiring adventure in unfolding the mystery of what represents man as the true image of the All Serene in humble representation of *sat, chit* and *ananda*. Life to be revealed in completeness demands activities to be performed amidst the overflow of 'the spring of culture' as Tagore identifies in terms of religion besides other ends-in-view in which man finds himself at ease with his gradual and spontaneous upbringing through education of the mind and the heart, the spirit and the soul.

To realise the inner significance of functions and festivals in terms of the religion of joy as Tagore remarkably expresses in his philosophy of religion is to have a new vision of fulfilment for which life always craves. It is a realisation of the greater 'I' which eliminates all narrowness and selfishness and endears the grandeur of the great and generous, the noble and the simple. The normal tendency among the partners of functions and festivals is to end up with the bankruptcy of the mind and the heart often consequential to our poverty reflected in boredom and fatigue. There is a certain sense of loneliness clubbed with bleakness and void as aftermath of functions and festivals. Tagore makes us alert of this poverty of mind and heart. He categorically refers to our inability to broaden our vision in the light of our diverse pitfalls associated with or reflected in our observations of what is great and what adds beauty and joy, wonder and askance to our life. In delving deep into the nature and purpose of functions and festivals, he makes an impressive and penetrating study of what grandeur is in terms of God and religion and elucidates how the two patterns of realisation apparent and intrinsic make significant contributions to one's religious sensibilities:

> Many a time we bankrupt ourselves by holding festivals. The day wanes in repaying debts alone. If a man with a meagre means wants to fulfil his desire to become a king for a day, then he bankrupts his ten days as he finds no alternative.
>
> For this reason the day after any festival is so colourless; on that day the brightness of the light of the sky goes out—the heart on that day becomes heavy with fatigue.
>
> But there is no way out. At least for a day in a year man wants to make a bond of relationship with the Affluent by eliminating his miserliness. He realises that God by dint of grandeur.
>
> There are two kinds of realisation: the one in which the poor understands the rich through accumulation of wealth. In such a pattern of realisation the very points of differences are

greatly realised. The second type of realisation is one of having the same ability. In that case, I do not have to sit outside the door. It is something like sitting, as it were, in the same cushion. Everyday when we exist poorly, the joyless mind is begging to the Joyful. He also wants to say on the day of the ceremony: 'Today it is not only giving, I would also like to be joyful like you. Today I have no poverty, no miserliness. My joy and sacrifice today are verily ample like you.'

In this way, if I feel within myself what grandeur is and what is called abundant affluence, I understand and prove that God is not only my master who blessed me with His favour but is also my relative.

—Rabindranath Tagore: "Santiniketan", *Rabindra-Rachanavali,* Government of West Bengal, Calcutta, Vol. XIV, 1992, pp. 682-683.

[Translated by me]

Probing deep into the priceless pleasures and poignancies of functions and festivals, Tagore identifies a new religion of man in which man makes a very colourful and candid relationship with the All Beautiful. He also makes inroads to what purifies and promotes one's ways of looking at and participating in functions and festivals not as a mere creed or credo but as a solemn march for grandeur of the mind and the heart promising catholicity of vision and encounter with the Ever Joyful.

Tagore also upholds a newer vision of religion which one practises and disseminates through close and sincere participation in functions and festivals. This is the religion of how to gradually and sincerely enrich and equip oneself to glorify and enrich the functions and festivals aimed at or to be celebrated today or tomorrow. In fact, every day, every moment as he categorically reminds us, is a day or a moment of functions and ceremonies. Therefore, there is no difference between an ordinary day and a day of festivals. Every day is an auspicious one to encounter the All Beautiful. Therefore, let each and every moment of every day be a thrilling and buoyant involvement in sincere devotion to preparing oneself to be justified to the All Beautiful by means of the exercise of joy in the true spirit of service in functions and festivals.

Tagore makes an altogether new approach to religion through functions and festivals when he advises us to assess and accelerate the latter in terms of identification of and involvement in every day as one of ceremonies. However, it is really a very difficult and arduous task in which we fail to show our best feats and accomplishments primarily because we fail to negotiate with the void created after every function and festival we take part, observe or enjoy. As Tagore characteristically elucidates:

> One who accumulates some resources everyday, one who goes on arranging some festivals, one who makes no total difference between the day of festivals and everyday but admits the bond of relationship between the two, encounters no sadness.
>
> If this does not take place, then we have to arrange festivals by accepting debts. We do enjoy ourselves but that enjoyment in most cases is not an outcome of our own but an

> almost totally borrowed one. The borrowings are in forms of congregations of people, garlands, lights, decoration, its other borrowings being songs, music and lectures. In the excitement of the day of festivals we fail to be conscious of the fact that everything is going on in debts. On the next day, when flowers become dry, lights extinguish and guests depart, then the enormous void of debt becomes visible and makes our hearts restless.
>
> For this very poverty on our part, we bid farewell to the god of festivals with the very inauguration. We make no arrangements to make the Lord of functions seated in the seat of everyday.
>
> —*Ibid.*, p. 683.

[Translated by me]

The emancipating and elevating influence of Nature as Tagore highlights in his philosophy of religion gives an altogether new direction to how Nature can be best endeared through functions and festivals where she becomes a part and parcel of meaningful, purposeful and living education. Why does Tagore want to vigorously introduce Nature through the daily routine of education? Why does he want to inspire in making a kinship with her? The reasons are obvious. First, Nature is what man is. This is to be idealised and practised. For idealisation and practice, love for Nature should be the essential end-in-view of education where functions and festivals are means to highlight this objective. This religion of love expressed, practised and disseminated by means of love of Nature leads significantly to love of man. Explaining the aims and objectives of education for children at Visva-Bharati, Tagore unfolds the spirit of religion that necessitates proper nurturing in course of participating in diverse functions and festivals which prompt one to appreciate the poignant vision of life:

> There is another aspect of child education of this place. It is to enable little boys and girls to understand the poignant and great significance of life. The slogan of devotional pursuit in our country is: whatever is great begets happiness; there is no happiness in littleness. But politics alone has now engulfed the whole arena of the great. My point is this: the greatest ideal of man will have to be introduced to children. This is why we pronounce here any great message of our ancient *tapovana* in the morning and in the evening and remain silently seated for a while. Whatever might be the outcome of this, there is some sort of confession. Through these functions, the little boys receive beckoning of the great. May be that they are moving their hands and feet while seated at the time of prayer or becoming restless, but a poignant significance of being seated in this seat reaches their mind day by day.
>
> My intention was: the boys of this place would fill in the prime time of their lives with diverse essence of enjoyments. The minds of children in constant association with Nature and in regular exercise of histrionics, drawing etc. in order to have an appreciation to the

> spirit of joy would be stored up with the reminiscence of joy in the sub-conscious state—keeping this view, I started my work.
>
> —Rabindranath Tagore: "Visva-Bharati", *Rabindra-Rachanavali,* Government of West Bengal, Calcutta, Vol. XIV, 1992, pp. 501-502.
>
> [Translated by me]

That religious education can be best imparted through Nature in an *ashram* atmosphere where there is an abundance of beauty and purity of Nature has been proved immensely successful by Tagore in his educational institutes at Santiniketan and Sriniketan. Why does he take recourse to the vastness of Nature and her purity, beauty and simplicity? Why does he think that the spirit of religion can be ideally and practically introduced in endearing and appreciating Nature in day-to-day education and, therefore, of life? As an incomparable exponent of universal religion, Tagore penetrates deep into the sub-conscious state of the human mind. The nature of the human mind is to yearn for the unknown and the infinite. The emotional sensibilities manifested in components like a longing for knowing the unknown and the infinite await a sincere and abiding kinship with Nature which is the essence of true religion. Therefore, the importance of the exercise of these components through Nature in functions and festivals can hardly be overestimated.

To associate oneself with the festivals of Nature and make kinship with her is to learn a new lesson of discipline which again conforms to the religion of sympathy and affinity, and this is what Tagore professes in his philosophy of religion. This religion has its three-fold aspect. First, with such religion observed through close association with Nature, the emotional sensibilities dormant and otherwise arrested find a vibrant avenue of emancipation. Second, this religion is simply the religion of freedom which acts as a remedy against violence, hatred and other psycho-social irregularities often exhibited in misguided and barred adolescence. Third, this religion of associating oneself with the rich and abundant festivities and ceremonies of Nature ensures furtherance of creative exercise and normal development of mind and body consequential to one's being hale and hearty.

Tagore adroitly refers to the facts as above in his own excellent observation:

> When mind and life are given full freedom, they achieve health. I adopted the system of freedom cure, if I can give it the name. The boys were allowed to run about, to climb difficult trees, and often to come to grief in their falls. They would get drenched in the rain; they would swim in the pond. Through Nature's own method, a cure came to the boys who were considered very bad; and when they returned home, their parents were surprised to find the immense change effected.
>
> —Rabindranath Tagore: "The Schoolmaster", *The Modern Review,* Calcutta, July, 1924.

With the beckoning of Nature amidst her rich ceremonies of joy, fear, hope, disappointment, happiness, sorrow, freedom etc. the religion of learning how to be identified and be in unison with the great universe becomes a living reality. The infinite call of Nature with all her passionate appeals to find out the mystery of life is an unending passion which always looks forward to a certain pattern of fulfilment by means of active participation in functions and festivals. Indeed, Tagore highlights the Infinite through Nature not as a mere ritual but as a purely religious vision which finds its manifestation as a passion negotiated in functions and festivals. When he speaks of Brahma as a religious faith, he discards all narrowness and sectarian outlook. Instead, he broadens the vision of the Infinite in every human being and widens the arena of joy. As a matter of fact, he wants to impart religious education by means of functions and festivals not rigorously by introducing books of scriptures or religion but by encouraging every learner to have a joyous realisation of the Infinite. All lessons on religion are thus transformed and transmitted as lessons of joy and other passionate experiences in human life where everyone cares not for the self but for the best well-being of all or altruism. Tagore's own clarification on how religious passion arises is relevant in this connection:

> The religious passion arises out of the most intimate, intense and incessant striving of man to remove the deepest sense of want in his soul.
>
> -Rabindranath Tagore: *Siksha,* Visva-Bharati, 1351 B.S., Vol. I, p. 142.

[Translated by H.B. Mukherjee: *Education for Fulness,* Asia Publishing Company, Bombay, 1962, p. 42]

That the passionate cry of the human soul wants an appropriate avenue of emancipation is the cry of the Infinite for which all functions and festivals have a very significant role. Tagore gives less importance to routine-ruled activities related to religion because these arrest freedom of mind and thought and also dwarf the joyous pursuit of religion as it appeals to an individual in all spontaneity and curiosity. Moreover, the religious education that he wants to impart actually fosters the spirit of making a joyous and creative adventure into the mysteries of human nature by synchronising with the mysteries of Nature. This is why functions and festivals are important as a living means for exercise of the human spirit.

Tagore's own experiences and experiments on religious education in an atmosphere of the *ashram* at Visva-Bharati where he joyously introduces different functions and festivals and where children discover the warmth of the mysteries which elevate the human soul in right religious pursuit in love with Nature may be recalled:

> What is really necessary is neither temples nor external rites and rituals. We want the *ashram,* where the clear beauty of Nature combined with the pure pursuits of human mind has created a sacred site for worthy endeavours. Nature and the human spirit wedded together shall constitute our temple, and selfless good deed our worship.* * * Such a spot, if found, shall provide the true atmosphere for religious education. For, as I have said before, according to the mysteries of human nature, religious education is possible only in the natural atmosphere of piety; all artificial means only pervert or abstract it.
>
> —*Ibid.,* p. 150.
>
> [Translated by me]

The main thrust that Tagore wants to imply through religion and, for that end-in-view, functions and festivals is that the latter are both intrinsically and extrinsically related to human growth and development. That religion makes a distinctive feature in all functions and festivals in Visva-Bharati till today with that spirit of human endeavour where everyone is concerned with religion not as a ritualistic, drab and dogmatic entity but a close and intense one in quest of man's ascent and excellence.

It is interesting to note in this connection how Tagore wants to infuse the true spirit of religion among people of Santiniketan by introducing programmes of activities related to the service for the neighbouring community which is still endeared as an ideal festival of discovery of right relationship with the neighbours through which they learn the religion of love and respect, sympathy and cooperation, devotion and dedication. While highlighting the role of students in practising religion as above, he appositely observes:

> There is not a single state in Bengal where, at different places, new religious communities are not being evolved among uneducated people. The educated people are never in the know of these. They never consider that an enormous community of masses is set afoot unnoticed. It is not true that they have remained seated because we do not look at them in indignity. The new spirit of the new era does actually go on working within them for change. It is not possible to know the country without knowing in which way that change is going on or what term it is conceiving.

I do not say that it is the ultimate aim to know the country. There is a significance to know well the actions and reactions of all human being whatsoever or howsoever. There is a learning in the endeavour of reading the living man directly by leaving books. As a consequence, one not only knows but also develops a spirit to know, which cannot at all be developed by reading in classes. If the pupils with the leadership of the Association can bring all the informatics related to the religious communities among the people of the lower classes in their own states, they would also receive the education to look at people with attention and, at the same time, would be able to serve the country also.

It is not that we do not read books on anthropology that is ethnology. But when we see that we do not feel the slightest form of enthusiasm to have a full-fledged account of the earthenware workers, cremation assistants, fishermen, weavers living beside us due to our bookish learning of that sort, then alone we can understand what a great superstition has grown up among ourselves about books, how great we consider books and how insignificantly we know about him who is reflected by means of books. But if once, by leaving all abstractions, we enter into the original abode of knowledge, there would be no end to our curiosity. If our pupils engage themselves well in all-round search of all these neighbours of theirs, there is no doubt that they would receive rewards of service in service itself.

—Rabindranath Tagore: *"Chhatrader Prati Sambhasan"* ("Address to Students"), *Siksha,* Visva-Bharati, 1973, pp. 24-25.

[Translated by me]

What transpires from the above is that Tagore wants to involve students in that kind of religion where the spirit of religion is reflected in the service of sincerity and love and not in ceremonies of religious rituals.

The spirit of participation exercised in the spirit of service to the despised and the downtrodden, the ignored and the hapless marks a newer vista of religion which Tagore wants to incorporate in every function and festival in a very succinct and crystallised manner. His dance dramas like *Shyama, Chitrangada* etc. convey the message of this new religion where the spirit of man is elevated and ennobled to attain that height of purity and poignancy which indicates the religion of man in fullness.

Why does Tagore want to highlight functions and festivals as the means of exercise of religion par excellence? It is simply because he feels in his heart of hearts the ever living presence of the All Beautiful, and so, bearing in mind the fact that human life in this world is transitory, he visualises death in the light of the world with all its 'careless treasures'. The religion that he wants to practise is to enter into the ceremony of the overlooked in order to re-enliven himself in the philosophy of timelessness. Such a religion is a great lesson that makes death a symbol of appreciation to the sky and the sun, the moon and the stars, the birds and the beasts, the plants and the trees and all other components of Nature where the ceremony of silence is buoyant with the ceremony of life:

> I know that the day will come when my sight of this earth shall be lost, and life will take its leave in silence, drawing the last curtain over my eyes.
>
> Yet stars will watch at night, and morning rise as before, and words heave like sea waves casting up pleasures and pains.
>
> When I think of this end of my moments, the barrier of the moments breaks and I see by the light of death thy world with its careless treasures. Rare is its lowest seat, rare is its meanest of lives.
>
> Things that I longed for in vain and things that I get—let them pass. Let me but truly possess the things that I ever spurned and overlooked.
>
> —Rabindranath Tagore: *Gitanjali,* Macmillan India Limited, New Delhi, Macmillan Pocket Tagore Edition, 1983, No. XCII, p. 61.

When comes such a religious visionary?

References

1. Adharmenaidhate tavat tato bhadran pacvati tatah sapatnan jayati samulastu vinacyati.

2. Pracantah
3. Yuktamanah

3

Religion and Joy: Tagorean Synchronisation

Unlike other religious thinkers, Rabindranath Tagore makes a significant point of departure in his philosophy of religion with a perfect blend of religion and joy. According to him, joy is the essence of religion which makes one enriched with the vision of inwardness to enter into the Holy Grail and to make oneself continually prepared to adore the Man of the Mind—*Maner Manush.*

Joy or *ananda* as Tagore endears in his religion of man is the 'indwelling light of truth' that encapsulates the vision of 'the eternal harmony of our own reality'. What harmony does he seek? It is the harmony of love and truth—*Satyam*—where joy makes an eternal bridge to visualise the All Beautiful. Unless one discovers this harmony and follows the path of truth, whatever joy one derives becomes artificial and transitory. The truth in one in unison with the truth in others becomes the real fountain of joy leading to the joy of encountering the All Serene. This also ensures 'the indwelling light' of the truth of oneness which brings man nearer to man. In Tagore's invaluable words:

By the indwelling light of this truth, I know that the world to which I belong, and which consists of an endless series of movements, has an inner truth of its own which is one, and which gives reality to the innumerable facts we know about the universe. We realise this inner truth, we experience *Ananda,* Joy, for through Joy we discover the eternal harmony of our own reality.

So often we ignore the real truth of a man and only deal with surface facts about him. The man who sells things to me is, for myself, a mere fact. The man whom I employ as my servant is a bundle of certain facts, all useful in the particular facts and circumstances of life. Through such facts I find the satisfaction of many of my needs, but no joy. For joy comes only when we realise the harmony of the *Satyam,* or Truth, that is in us, with the *Satyam,* or Truth, that is in others, and, in this case, in my servant. But with regard to our loved ones, we are directly aware of the deeper truth which is constantly manifested through them in their outer life, because with them we more easily realise a mutual affinity. Their outer activity may hold no value for own life's purposes. May it even be a hindrance. They have, however, an ultimate value for us in that they are, that they embody, an inner truth which is also within me.

—Rabindranath Tagore: "The Philosophical Approach to Santiniketan", L. K. Elmhirst: *Rabindranath Tagore: Pioneer in Education,* Visva-Bharati, 1961, p. 86.

To explore the inner truth, the joy that awaits efflorescence in action and appreciation is an altogether new dimension in Tagore's religious philosophy. He adores joy in life in order to eliminate 'bondage of action' and see life in all its aroma of perfection. Therein lies the joy of freedom. Therein also lies the joy to appreciate the mystery of life well expressed in the mystery of Nature. True religion as expressed in joy also makes a happy blending of freedom, action, joy and life to have a perfect realisation of the Infinite. Taking cues from the Upanishads on the philosophy of action, Tagore elucidates how joy helps one realise the true role of action in order to have a true realisation of the Infinite:

> The Upanishad says: *In the midst of activity alone wilt thou desire to live a hundred years.*[1] It is the saying of those who had amply tasted the joy of the soul. Those who have fully realised the soul have never talked in mournful accents of sorrowfulness of life or of the bondage of action. They are not like the weakling flower whose stem-hold is so light that it drops away before attaining fruition. They hold on to life with all their might and say, 'never will we let go till the fruit is ripe.' They desire in their joy to express themselves strenuously in their life and in their work. Pain and sorrow dismay them not, they are not bowed down to the dust by the weight of their own heart. With the erect head of the victorious hero they march through life seeing themselves and showing themselves in increasing resplendence of the soul through both joys and sorrows. The joy of their life keeps step with the joy of that energy which is playing at

> building and breaking throughout the universe. The joy of the sunlight, the joy of the free air, mingling with the joy of their lives, makes one sweet harmony reign within and without. It is they who say, *In the midst of activity alone wilt thou desire to live a hundred years.*
>
> This joy of life, this joy of work, in man is absolutely true. It is no use saying that it is a delusion of ours; that unless we cast it away we cannot enter upon the path of self-realisation. It will never do the least good to attempt the realisation of the Infinite apart from the world of action.
>
> —Rabindranath Tagore: "Realisation in Action", *Sadhana,* Macmillan India Limited, New Delhi, Macmillan Pocket Tagore Edition, 1983, pp. 103-104.

Tagore further believes in the existence of this universe with all beings and things created from joy. As such, he strongly upholds the saying of the Upanishads that their created universe is the creation of joy: *Anandadhyeva khalvimani bhutani jayante.* How to be an eternal partner of joy? How to be in unison with Brahma? It is through our perfection by means of realisation of action in the spirit of joy. The strings of the harp are to be well attuned in the spirit of the joy of freedom. Thus any action accomplished in the joy of freedom makes it meaningful, purposeful, relevant and poignant for realisation of the All Serene. Our quest for *dharma* and truth always awaits our continual and devoted strivings for tuning ourselves perfectly with the song of freedom, the song of the soul which is the song of joy. And this song should always be associated with every work anywhere and everywhere. Our striving should be to make a ceaseless journey towards the path of the joy of freedom by steadfastly holding truth aloft so that the kingdom of God within each one of us be resplendent with the radiance of joy in complete renunciation of desires that stand in the way of union with the All Serene. Tagore adroitly elucidates his philosophy of the religion of the joy of freedom as follows:

> The truth has its law, it has its joy. On one side of it is being chanted the *Bhayadasyagnistapati,*[2] on the other the *Anandadhyeva khalvimani bhutani jayante*[3]. Freedom is impossible of attainment without submission to law, for Brahma is one aspect bound by his truth, in the other free in his joy.
>
> As for ourselves, it is only when we wholly submit to the bonds of truth that we fully gain the joy of freedom. And how? As does the string that is bound to the harp. When the harp is truly strung, when there is not the slightest laxity in the strength of the bond, then only does music result; and the string transcending itself in its melody finds at every chord its true freedom. It is because it is bound by such hard and fast rules on the one side that it can find this range of freedom in music on the other. While the string was not true, it was indeed merely bound; but a loosening of its bondage would not have been the way to freedom, which it can fully achieve by being bound tighter till it has attained its true pitch.

> The bass and treble strings of our duty are only bonds so long as we cannot maintain them steadfastly attuned according to the law of truth; and we cannot call by the name of freedom the loosening of them into the nothingness of inaction. That is why I would say that the true striving in the quest for truth, of *dharma,* consists not in the neglect of action but in the effort to attune it closer and closer to the eternal harmony. The text of this striving should be, *Whatever works thou doest, consecrate them to Brahma.*[4] That is to say, the soul is to dedicate itself to Brahma through all its activities. This dedication is the song of the soul, in this is its freedom. Joy reigns when all work becomes the path to the union with Brahma; when the soul ceases to return constantly to its own desires; when in it our self-offering grows more and more intense. Then there is completion, then there is freedom, then, in this world, comes the kingdom of God.
>
> —*Ibid.*, pp. 108-109.

Tagore makes joy a religion and course of action synchronised with the religion of love. The realisation of religion in terms of joy and love, well synchronised to make a trio of joy, love and freedom, makes religion a symbol of Truth, Goodness and Beauty. In fact, he adores the All Joy as an ever present all pervading comrade who has taught how to realise His presence:

> Stealthily do thou comest in the dark night,
> Thou art my friend
> And clasp me in strong hands,
> Thou art my joy.

Thou art my lone charioteer of the chariot of sorrow,
Thou art my friend alone.
Thou art the crisis, loss thou art,
Thou art my joy.
An enemy am I, win me over,
Thou art my friend alone.
Furious thou art, the fear of fears,
Thou art my joy.
Come, ye thunder, tearing off the breast,
Thou art my friend alone.
Take, ye death, breaking off the barriers,
Thou art my joy.

—Rabindranath Tagore: *Rabindra-Rachanavali,* Government of West Bengal, Calcutta, 1987, Vol. V, p. 360.

[Translated by me]

With an optimistic approach to life, Tagore welcomes joy as the religion of man's ever vibrant march for fullness. This approach has enabled him to welcome Spring as the embodiment of All Joy who teaches him how to be victorious against all trials and tribulations of life in its manifold effulgence as the pollens of *Nagkeshar* flowers spread the fragrance in the restless wind. As he muses:

Come, Spring, come to the earth,
Bring new tunes again and again.
Bring new life, new songs,
Bring idle breeze burdened with the fragrance of wine.
Bring poignant consciousness in every heart of the universe
Bring new waves of excitement,
Bring, bring on earth the movement of the rhyme joyous,

Break, break the fetters of chains,
Bring, bring the pains of boisterous heart on earth
Come in the mildly trembled,
Enamoured with murmurs,
Joyous with new leaves—
Eager for flowers in the garden of *malati* creepers
In the shadow of happiness, in the air sweet,
Come, eager for blooming,
Come, the ever interested.
The eternal traveller in the garden of heaven,
Bring the flute-resonant night for unison,
Come with the full brimmed cup of wine in your hands,
Come in the lap of dawn in the lotus coloured sun's feet
Come in the enchanted moonlit night,
Come in the serene cottage of flowers
In the water of the lake asleep in happiness
Come like flashes of lightning in the dance of hailstorm
In the surging waves of the sea,
Come in the morn thrilled with awakening,
Come in cities, fields and forests,
Come in words, speech and mind,
Come with steps humming with the sound of *manjira,*
Come with the voice chirping with the sound of music,
Come with the sweet garland of *mallika,*
Come with the dress of tender new leaves,
Come, beautiful, in the speed of youth,
Come, the emboldened here, in new prayer,

O unvanquished, make the victorious journey,
March on in the war against disease and defeat,
Spreading the pollens of *nagkeshar*,
Waving the restless wind!

—Rabindranath Tagore: *Chitrangada*, *Rabindra-Rachanavali*, Government of West Bengal, Calcutta, 1987, Vol. IV, pp. 654-655.

[Translated by me]

For a serene encounter with the All Joy, Tagore makes the world nearer to the heart of man to proclaim a new religion which is the religion of love. This religion envisages one world of attuning oneself with the freedom of simplicity and modesty where everyone finds an ideal atmosphere of living with and loving Nature who becomes the voice of the inner man. This voice of the inner man overshadows sorrow, loss or pain and heralds the victory of man with the principles and practice of the religion of self-crystallisation in quest of joy.

Coming down to the realities of life, Tagore exposes the religion of togetherness of being in unity with everyone in and around us which highlights the joy of living in the true sense of the term. He is shocked at the degeneration of religion in the appalling alienation of man from the world of joy by dissociating himself from the society. The joy that emanates from education and life is the one that synchronises the one with the other and such a synchronisation between education and life is the fountain of the religion of joy.

To sincerely respond to each 'I' in order to have a real taste of joy in all 'We' and vice versa is the religion which Tagore wants to disseminate by means of living education, for he earnestly believes that the infinite spirit of man finds delight in sympathy and cooperation which are the invaluable components of every religion. In his seminal essay *'Sikshar Herpher"* ("Topsy-turvy in Education"), he concludes by drawing our attention to the yet-to-be-adorned religion of unison between education and life which indicates how we can successfully practise the religion of joy:

> Being dissociated, man is becoming a failure. He cannot stand up strong by achieving an indivisible pattern of unity within himself. He is not getting anything necessary for him within the reach at the appropriate point of time. There is a story. When a poor man would purchase winter garments by saving little by little during winter, the summer season would in the meantime step in. Again, when he would be able to procure light dresses by striving throughout the summer season, the early winter would set in. When, seeing his poverty, the Almighty became merciful and wanted to bless him with a boon, he said, 'Nothing more do I want. Please do away with this topsy-turvy. If you make a slight correction so that I might receive garments of summer and winter at the appropriate time, I think my life would be meaningful.'
>
> We have also the same prayer. If the differences are eliminated, we are contented. We have this appalling poverty because we are failing to make conformity between winter and garments of winter, summer and garments for

> summer. Otherwise, everything we have. Now we pray to the Almighty for this boon: synchronise our appetite with food, clothes with seasons, ideas with language and education with life.
>
> —Rabindranath Tagore: "*Sikshar Herpher*" ("Topsy-turvy in Education"), *Siksha,* Visva-Bharati, 1973, pp. 18-19.
>
> [Translated by me]

Life bereft of the cultivation of the religion of joy is, as Tagore more often than not reminds us, life sans religion. As all religions aim at enrichment of the mind and the soul, the sky of the mind and the heart demand a joyous involvement in every action and contemplation. Such an involvement brings us in close harmony with everyone within and around us. Then, and then only, we can make a journey from 'I' to 'We' and vice versa. Then, and then only, we respond and respect the desire of the self and the existence of the self everywhere from true religious perspectives. Tagore welcomes us to celebrate and nurse joy as an inseparable part of religion from these perspectives where the religion of every society is pulsating with the religion of joy:

> Our real significance is not within ourselves. That is spread over everything in this world. That is why we are seeking for that everything continually with all our intelligence and with all our actions. We are always craving for unison with everything. Otherwise, we fail to have ourselves within us. The only desire of the self is to realise the self everywhere.

* * *

Likewise, we would visualise ourselves as existent everywhere, and, if this is so, we would then truly visualise ourselves. The more extensively would we know about the self, the more would we have joy. Whoever pulls himself off from within and manifests in a truer fashion is considered to be our relative. He alone gives us joy.

For this very reason, the only original significance within the creation of the houses, the society, the state whatsoever made by the human soul from time immemorial is that by giving up the loneliness of an individual, man would realise himself in a greater sphere by means of extending his diverse strength in numerous relationship among the legion and the diverse, and this is his real happiness. And, for this, it is said: *'Bhumaiva sukham nalpe sukhamasti'*—vastness is happiness, no happiness is there in littleness. It is because of littleness that the soul also becomes paltry.

—Rabindranath Tagore: "Santiniketan", *Rabindra-Rachanavali,* Government of West Bengal, Calcutta, Birth Centenary Edition, 1961, Vol. XI, p. 144.

[Translated by me]

'To stand at the innermost centre of things', as Tagore prescribes for 'fulness of disinterested joy' is the essence of religion. Such religion brings nearer to Brahma, the All Joyful and we are blessed with the catholic spirit of beauty and love. In fact, the religion that we seek through joy is one of perfect blissfulness of beauty which ensures us to realise the spectacular cohesion of the universe. Goodness and love are then the prominent and pure components of our religion where joy unendingly exists and pervades the human mind. The heart also exalts in beauty and joy and prepares for union with Brahma. The search for beauty and truth intermingled with each other is actually the search for the religion of joy that allows us to emancipate. While elucidating the finer elements of realisation of beauty, Tagore exposes this religion of disinterested joy:

> Through our sense of truth we realise law in creation, and through our sense of beauty we realise harmony in the universe. When we recognise love in nature we extend our mastery over physical forces and become powerful; when we recognise the law in our moral nature, we attain mastery over self and become free. In like manner the more we comprehend the harmony in the physical world the more our life shares the gladness of creation, and our expression of beauty in art becomes more truly catholic. As we become conscious of the harmony in our soul, our apprehension of the blissfulness of the spirit of the world becomes universal, and the expression of beauty in our life moves in goodness and love towards the infinite. This is the ultimate object of our existence, that we must ever know that 'beauty is truth, truth beauty'; we must realise the whole world in love, for love gives its birth, sustains it, and takes it back to its bosom. We

> must have that perfect emancipation of heart which gives us the power to stand at the innermost centre of things and have the taste of that fulness of disinterested joy which belongs to Brahma.
>
> —Rabindranath Tagore: "Realisation of Beauty", *Sadhana,* Macmillan India Limited, New Delhi, Macmillan Pocket Tagore Edition, 1983, p. 120.

The religion that Tagore highlights through joy is the joy of the soul. Such religion is above all narrowness, blindness, artificiality and abject emotionalism. It is the religion to make an unending adventure to find himself, his immortal self. This, indeed, is a joyous adventure because, in the end, it indicates that we are conscious of becoming 'one with the All'. Taking cues from the Upanishads, Tagore exquisitely exposes this religion of the cosmos—the religion to be 'one with the All'—and deliberates how the adventure of man towards the discovery of the soul is an adventure into the world of joy for emancipation from all constraints by means of 'the ceremony of the discipline of self-restraint and high thinking':

> To know our soul apart from the self is the first step towards the realisation of the supreme deliverance. We must know with absolute certainty that essentially we are spirit. This we can do by winning mastery over self, by rising above all pride and greed and fear, by knowing that worldly losses and physical death can take nothing away from the truth and the greatness of our soul. The chick

> knows when it breaks through the self-centred isolation from its egg that the hard shell which covered it so long was not really a part of its life. That shell is a dead thing, it has no growth, it affords no glimpse whatever of the vast beyond that lies outside it. However pleasantly perfect and rounded it may be, it must be given a blow to, it must be burst through and thereby the freedom of light and air be won, and the complete purpose of bird life be achieved. In Sanskrit, the bird has been called the twice-born: so too the man is named, who has gone through the ceremony of the discipline of self-restraint and high thinking for a period of at least twelve years; who has come out simple in wants, pure in heart, and ready to take up all the responsibilities of life in a disinterested largeness of spirit. He is considered to have had his rebirth from the blind envelopment of self to the freedom of soul life; to have come into living relation with his surroundings; to have become at one with the All.
>
> —*Ibid.*, pp. 25-26.

Tagore further exposes the journey towards realisation of soul in order to realise the religion of joy which is the religion of the soul:

> Man's history is the history of his journey to the unknown in quest of the realisation of his immortal self—his soul. Through the rise and fall of empires; through the building up gigantic piles of wealth and the ruthless scattering of them upon the dust; through the

creation of vast bodies of symbols that give shape to his dreams and aspirations, and the casting of them away like the playthings of an outworn infancy; through his forging of magic keys with which to unlock the mysteries of creation, and through his throwing away of this labour of ages to go back to his workshop and work up afresh some new form; yes, through it all man is marching from epoch to epoch towards the fullest realisation of his soul—the soul which is greater than the things man accumulates, the deeds he accomplishes, the theories he builds; the soul whose onward course is never checked by death or dissolution. Man's mistakes and failures have by no means been trifling or small, they have strewn his path with colossal ruins; his sufferings have been immense, like birth-pangs for a giant child; they are the prelude of a fulfilment whose scope is infinite. Man has gone through and is still undergoing martyrdoms in various ways, and his institutions are the altars he has built whereto he brings his daily sacrifices, marvellous in kind and stupendous in quantity. All this world be absolutely unmeaning and unbearable if all along he did not feel that deepest joy of the soul within him, which tries its divine strength by suffering and proves its exhaustless riches by renunciation.

—*Ibid.*, pp. 27-28.

Tagore adores the religion of joy not simply as a wayward journey from trivialities of life but makes life emancipated from all abstractions. He muses on the emancipation of the soul because therein lies the boundless sky of joy that proclaims the victory of man. The spirit of beauty in which he seeks the spirit of joy heralds the religion of man in the beyonding of unison of love and the longings of the lover and the beloved. What a swing from earthly joy to joy eternal and mystic! Here is a classic example:

> Darkness came in
> The birds slept
> The golden sunlight was in unison with the sky
> The clouds devastated towards eternity
> And the main swing a-sitting.
> Come closer to the breast each other
> In fusion with each other's mouth
> Endearing with arms
> Slowly is the breath falling
> Now and then with intervals,
> Looking at the sky they behold
> The two stars at the backdrop of the tree
> Where does the heart fly, O where,
> It rushes towards those stars it gets lost in the sky.
> Leaving the earth
> They have, as it were, become two stars.

—Rabindranath Tagore: *"Dola"* ("The Swing"), *Chhabi O Gaan, Rabindra-Rachanavali,* Government of West Bengal, Calcutta, 1980, Vol. I, p.123.

[Translated by me]

Probing deep into the mystery of life, Tagore presents us with the joy that promises a new religion, a new askance and a new vision of eternal poignancy. He, in joy, fully toys with life as a playhouse but at the same time hints at the everlasting joy of life which purifies and proclaims life with the fragrance of vastness. The romantic spirit of love adorned in the splashing joy of the playhouse turns into an endless aura of reminiscence with all serenity and catholicity that true religion always brings forth:

> Who are making us play in our play-house?
> Ere the play is over, we came back in the eve
> Where have you thrown that room of dust away?
> Here where we two sat
> The heavenly union of laughter and tears was made,
> What a sea of words we wrote by tracing on the sand,
> Who are you that wiped out those endearing writings?
> The sweet girl will roll on the ground here,
> When kissed, her smile would spread abloom
> For what the *madhavi* creeper raised her head here,
> Thought I, she would for ever remain abloom
> O where and who has trampled her!

—Rabindranath Tagore: *"Bhavishyater Rangabhumi"* ("The Playground of the Future"), *Kadi O Kamal, Rabindra-Rachanavali,* Government of West Bengal, Calcutta, 1980, Vol. I, p. 202.

[Translated by me]

When Tagore explores joy out of beauty, he also explores the religion of beauty and joy amidst the mystery of Nature. This is characteristically represented in his poem *"Vimvavati"* where, in a setting of dramatic contrast, he brings out the essence of beauty in the silent joy of affluence in simplicity and austerity:

The golden headgear the Queen began to rub
With sand. The reflection still remained
She besmeared with ink but unaffected the picture was
She trimmed fire in it, but the gold melt not.
She threw it on the ground with tremendous force.
But the mystic mirror broke not. On the ground
The Queen suddenly fell down and life came to an end
The diamonds and the jewels like fire
Began to burn. Beside her on the ground
Two laughing faces smile in her golden mirror—
Vimvavati, the step daughter of the Queen,
The most beautiful of all on earth

—Rabindranath Tagore: *"Vimvavati"*, *Sonar Tari*, *Rabindra-Rachanavali*, Government of West Bengal, Calcutta, 1980, Vol. I, p. 440.

[Translated by me]

The quest for joy arising out of the quest for beauty as Tagore makes in his creative endeavour introduces us with a religion of self-revelation and self-discovery. True to his religion and joy, he makes a frank statement in words of poetry about his intention of creative exercise. As he characteristically unfolds himself:

Amid this silent mind often sounds
The wavy stroke of the world
Therefore, in the sounding heart no rest is there
Sleepless are the day and the night
The voice of songs of joy and sorrow is continually heard

The sound alone, and no language is there
The manifold murmur makes me restless,
Manifold vain hope does me awake,
And so all thro' this life I have nothing to do
Save composing the limit of the endless
With hope and language, pouring love with them,
I build up the image of my mind.

—Rabindranath Tagore: *"Upahar"* ("The Gift"), *Manasi, Rabindra-Rachanavali,* Government of West Bengal, Calcutta, 1980, Vol. I, p. 303.

[Translated by me]

The joy of endearing sounds in Nature that Tagore seeks, enjoys and appreciates is the joy of the mind and the heart, where the image of the All Beautiful opens a new chapter in the religion of man. He makes a thrilling quest for joy, for instance, in the poem *"Pratidhvani"* ("The Echo") where he makes a sonorous journey from this world to the kingdom of Beauty of the All Serene quite dramatically and ultimately conjoins himself in eternal bondage with the wonder of the echo:

O Echo
I understand I love you
I understand I love none else
You may have made me eager and restless
My *veena* weeps for you
Hearing the songs of birds in your mouth
The murmuring of the fountain
The song of the intense mysterious forest
The pleasant voice of the lad
Hearing from you the music of the world
I have loved you
Yet, do I not see you?
I have sought you throughout the world.

* * * * * *

Until death, unendingly shall I seek you,
Shall I not have your trace?
Will you remain away, from a very great distance,
Shall I not hear that faint music?
Standing amid this world
The flute of beauty will you play on
In the endless track of life shall I go on
Seeking you,
Vacant will be the heart and the mind.

—Rabindranath Tagore: *"Pratidhvani"* ("The Echo"), *Prabhat Sangeet, Rabindra-Rachanavali,* Government of West Bengal, Calcutta, 1980, Vol. I, pp. 80-83.

[Translated by me]

The romantic fusion of love and joy as Tagore makes in his creative endeavour has a serene backdrop of religion which has an elegant ambience in being born and burnt in the intoxication of love. Why does he make such a fusion? Perhaps he idealises joy to be purified in love, which is an efflorescence of the All Love. Here is a panoramic scene of the lover and the beloved creating an atmosphere of divine joy amidst a drowsy canvas where the religion of love and joy makes a serene aura of the depth of vision and life.

Let's go to the river-bank
Sitting there slowly
Do you play on a flute only
The moon will smile in the sky
In your sweet voice slowly
Do you sing a song of happiness only.

* * * *

O maiden, by singing

Do you keep weaving the garland of *malati*
While asleep, garland him.
The fragrance of the flowers will unite in dream
Keep staring at the sleeping face with love
The mild smile will flower in the face.

—Rabindranath Tagore: *"Matal"* ("The Intoxicated"), *Chhabi O Gaan, Rabindra-Rachanavali,* Government of West Bengal, Calcutta, 1980, Vol. I, p. 135.

[Translated by me]

Tagore makes a haunting search for joy amidst Nature not because she appeals extrinsically with all her beauty and love but essentially because he finds in her an endless sphere of eternity in the simple but thrilling panorama of life well synchronised in the religion of nearness. A mellow atmosphere of joy tinged with the reminiscence of love makes life more in tune with the beckoning of the All Serene. As he exquisitely marches on the joy of reminiscence in all serenity for time future:

Where is the shadow of the tree, the green affection of the forest?
Embracing the trees on the banks with ripples all day long
Away towards the lovely home does the stream advance.
Where is the shadow of the tree, the green affection of the forest?
Where in the deep blue the end of the forest is in unison
The eyes lose vision in the endless sphere of eternity
The wind comes from the distance and away goes to the distant land
The muse goes a-floating, where do they go!

The laughter, the flute, and the jokes, the pure happy breaths
The union all the year on the green banks of the stream
Some play of swing or sleep on the lap of shadow
The day runs on towards the rippling stream
Some pluck *vakul,* some prepare the garland.
Like a shade in the shadow some go on singing,
Someone is whispering somewhere,
The hair is dishevelled, she has forgotten to know
She has held aloft in fingers lest the eyes are covered
The bangle is dropped, she is keeping in the shadow of the tree
Amid the forest murmur the lonely flute plays on
With that tuning sing the two doves at times.

—*Ibid., "Vaner Chhaya"* ("The Shadow of the Forest"), p. 203.

[Translated by me]

The Eliotean philosophy of Time present, Time past and Time future has a dramatic echo in Tagore as above but what makes the latter more intensive and appealing is his catholicity of vision where the religion of reminiscence breaks all barriers of Time and makes Time unendingly arresting and joyful as the religion of love. Love and joy unfold the religion of a new order, a new world where one seeks and seeks frantically the endless sphere of eternity.

The joy of love which Tagore introduces as the endless joy of religion finds an exponent in Malati, the Poet's sister, who becomes the darling of every family. The joy of love gets a rude shock but that very shock unveils a new horizon of joy, the hemlock of new fulfilment where life is enriched with the religion of love purged off from affection to bring forth the dawn of a new lotus-land of purity and poignancy:

O poisonous, fiery, thunderous love,
Cover your face before this affection!
The insect of death you are, the Satan of life,
Like fire you are in the beauteous forest of flowers,
Disease of the heart, you nurse
Thirst of in the heart of all the time.
Encompassing the snakelike clasping of your head
You go on breathing out poisonous air,
Fired with your volcanic breath
The heated current of blood blooms on!

* * * *

This love, this poison, this thundering fire—
When would these bid farewell to this earth?
Come ye, affection, come showering your pleasant stream of juice
Put out this burning heap of fire!
From the fiery clasp of the scorpion
Take up in your lap drenched with juice.
Yonder in the sky the comet of love is up
Flashing the eye, alas, of youth!
Where are you, the Pole Star, rise for once,
Pour in these burning eyes your lustre pleasant and soft,
Hemlock you are, a shadow, the stream of moonlight,
A rivulet, the air of the dawn,
Laughter you are, hope and tears mild.
Come and put out this love.
One who has one *Malati* in his family
A thousand *Damini* is not equal to her bowl of dust!

—*"Vish O Sudha", Sandhyasangeet, Ibid.,* pp. 55-56.

[Translated by me]

The exercise of joy as an inseparable component of religion finds poignancy in Tagore's symbolic vision of Beauty for which he is always ready to make an endless journey. He asks and asks how he would be able to probe into the deepest mystery of Beauty. The eternal silence he embraces in his askance makes him further prepared for a journey to the unknown and the endless. In his *"Niruddes Yatra"* ("The Journey to the Unknown"), he unfolds the religion of joy fathomed and purged in the religion of Beauty:

How far away would you take along, O Beautiful?
Tell me on which bank your golden boat would embark
When asked, O alien,
Smile you alone, O sweet smiling one,
I understand not what you feel within your mind.
Silently you show me by raising your finger.
The shoreless sea is surging,
Yonder is the western sun setting in the horizon of the sky,
What is here? In whose quest am I marching onward?

—*"Niruddes Yatra"* ("The Journey to the Unknown"), *Ibid.*, p. 541.

[Translated by me]

The joy that Tagore unfolds as above in self-askance and self-enquiry and makes a new emblem of religion becomes more suggestive with the cry of endless tears where the vision of the All Beautiful merges in the vision of love. The Poet seeks a sombre message—the message of the religion of joy and love crystallised with a new awakening:

Where the night mingles
With the sea of the day
On that juncture we two
Did unite,
The black and the white
Are in unison there
With darkness and light,
There the waves are running
Between the shores
Amid depthless blue silence
The sombre message played on
Unalloyed did bloom
The line of gold—
I prepare to look at the face
I am about to see but cannot see
I awake enraptured with dream
I cry with unending tears.

—*Geetimalya, Ibid.,* Vol. II, No. 1, p. 29.

[Translated by me]

The concept of beauty as the embodiment of All Joy makes us acquainted with a serene world of silence adorned with the religion of awe and adoration. In a religio-mystic personification of beauty where Tagore looks inwardly into the world of wonder and awe, the sensitising muse laves an unparalleled aroma of the quest for joy:

Beauty, you came in the morning today
With sun-hued *parijat* in your hands,
The sleeping castle, no passenger on the way
In the golden chariot you left alone
Stooping for a while towards the window

You glanced with your eyelids plaintive
Beauty, you came in the morning today.

In what fragrance was my dream filled,
In what joy the darkness of the room trembled,
Silent is my *veena* that trampled in the dust,
And with that unwounded stroke did it play on.

Many a time was I about to rise,
Leaving indolence run out towards the way .
When I awoke, you departed.
No more, I think, would we meet again,
Beauty, you came in the morning today.

—*"Geetanjali", Ibid.,* No. 51, p. 234.

[Translated by me]

Quite unassuming in his religion of joy, Tagore broadens the horizon of religion in simple and carefree events and matters of life and Nature—the sun, the spring, rains, shadows, the wind, and moments simple but soulful. This elevates the vision of All Joy anew and afresh:

My joy lies in seeing
Along the path
The sunshine and the shadow
Play on
The rains and the spring
Arrive
Who comes and goes
In front of me
Bringing the message
Pleased am I within me.
Gently blows the wind

With eyes wide open
Shall I remain alone in the door
When all on a sudden
The auspicious moment will come?
The meeting will take place.
Meanwhile, at times,
I sing and smile aside.
By then, at intervals,
The beautiful fragrance floats along,
Seeing along the path
Does my joy exist.

—"*Geetimalya*", *Ibid.*, p. 300

[Translated by me]

Why does Tagore adore joy in the religion of fullness? Why does he make a fusion of joy and beauty? There are definitely some aspects in his vision of joy and beauty as inseparable components of his philosophy of religion. He not only welcomes beauty as a joy of happiness but also welcomes it as an evolving force of looking within and finding out the treasures of sorrow in tears which are abiding objects of self-crystallisation. He expresses his indebtedness to beauty as joy in tears of sorrow from a new dimension of fullness which makes religion an entity of one's very own. As he remarkably delineates:

O Beautiful, you have brought tears
Welled up in eyes,
You have amid your breast
The fire of penance unbearable
And so sorrow shines in brilliance
The bonds of life enamoured are torn apart

With this heat does pulsate in efflorescence
The lotus of incoherence!

—*"Asru"* ("Tears"), *Mahua, Ibid.,* p. 841.

[Translated by me]

Freedom, too, finds in Tagore a new revelation of the religion which he seeks through joy. Joy here mingles in fullness whereby his creation finds a unison with the Creator. As he adroitly portrays:

With manifold image Freedom comes to many a person
And not with a single one,
The wine of fullness flows from world to world
In various tastes and diverse currents
Where my creation mingles with the Creator, I am
There bounded
Freedom responds to me in the midst of
Music mine!

—*"Mukti"* ("Freedom"), *Puravi, Ibid.,* pp. 641-642.

[Translated by me]

Tagore finds joy as the sonorous grandeur of beauty where the tumultuous passion of Nature gives a sudden jolt in the sparkling parade of imageries. What transpires from such a dramatic turn is the vision of beauty born of joy purified in the halo of the All Serene. Let us enjoy how he baptises us with the religion of joy in the dazzling light of beauty:

It is like a diamond in the middle of the ring
Made of platinum,

The clouds encompassing the horizon of the sky,
With the midway gap the field flashes with sunlight,
Terrific blows the wind.
Terror-stricken are the papaya plants,
Rebellion starts in the northern field among the *neem* trees,
A sea of scolding sweeps over the heads of the palm trees.

—*"Sundar", Punascha, Ibid.,* Vol. III, p. 25.

[Translated by me]

Turning towards human life, Tagore exposes the intrinsic beauty of joy in the vision of existence and dynamism, which unveils the religion of what we consider to be an invaluable gift from the All Serene: it is love. Unlike real life, where dedication and acceptance are poles apart, in love the two unite in the harmony of joy derived from fusion which alone persists as the eternal blessing of the All Serene.

Tagore also allows us to harmonise joy and religion in the very concept of the All Serene as Brahma by making inroads through the exercise of joy which is also the exercise of love. Such an exercise dispels all distance between the All Serene and each 'I' in the presence of the Divine I: call it Love Divine or Joy Divine. But, then, it wins over the challenge of the mind and the thought juxtaposed in the barrels of inaccessibility towards the All Serene.

Admittedly, Tagore traces the nature of man which supports a healthy synchronisation between joy and religion where love acts as an indwelling light in all splendour. As he characteristically elucidates:

In the world of work, sacrifice and gain belong to different categories—they are of different strata. In love, sacrifice and gain are one and the same. The very gift is a gain to whom we love. In the ledger of the accounts of joy, receipts and payments are in the same place. There receipts are the same as payments. In the creation of God in this feast of joy, whatever playoff love He has introduced is to achieve Him by Himself. To make one with this offering and receiving is called love.

* * * * *

The western philosophy observes: we have endless advancements—we continually advance towards Him but never go to Him. Our Upanishad says: we both go and do not go to Him. We either encounter Him or not. *Yato vacho nivartante aprapya manasa saha—anandam brahmano vidvan na vibheti kutacchana.* Nowhere such a queer and antithetical statement in the two lines of a *sloka* has been so clearly heard. Not only do words come back baffled but the mind also without having Him—this is an outright reply. And yet, he who knows the joy of Brahma is free from all fear. Then alone One who cannot be known at all is so known that there is no fear from anything. What knowing is referred to that? It is the knowing of joy, of love. This knowing by crossing over all what is unknown.

—Rabindranath Tagore: "*Santiniketan*", *Rabindra-Rachanavali,* Government of West Bengal, Calcutta, 1992, Vol. XIV, p. 663.

[Translated by me]

Delving deep into the human nature, Tagore exposes the world of joy and makes reference to the invaluable words of the Upanishads *Anadarupamamritam yadvibhati*—the immortal being manifests in the form of joy. The religion makes the highest contribution to the religion of man because all progress is the outcome of joy. In his own words:

> It indeed seems to be wonderful that nature has these two aspects at one and the same time, and so antithetical—one being of thraldom and the other of freedom. In the same form, sound, colour and taste two contrary notes are heard, one of necessity and the other of joy. Outwardly nature is busy and restless, inwardly she is all silence and peace. She has toil on one side and leisure on the other. You see her bondage only when you see her from without, but within her heart is a limitless beauty.
>
> Our seer says, 'From joy are born all creatures, by joy they are sustained, towards joy they progress, and into joy they enter.'
>
> —Rabindranath Tagore: "Realisation in Love", *Sadhana,* Macmillan India Limited, New Delhi, 1988, pp. 85-86.

The journey from the finite to the infinite and vice versa in religion through joy is what makes joy as the fountain of human advancement. Tagore points out this spirit of joy as the ever present endeavour of a creative artist who is always in the quest for the infinite and All Serene. Explaining this vision of joy, he observes:

> *The immortal being manifests himself in joy-form.*[5] His manifestation in creation is out

of his fullness in joy. It is the nature of this abounding joy to realise itself in form which is law. The joy, which is without form, must create, must translate into forms. The joy of the singer is expressed in the form of a song, that of the poet in the form of a poem. Man in his role of a creator is ever creating forms, and they come out of his abounding joy.

This joy, whose other name is love, must by its very nature have duality for its realisation. When the singer has his inspiration he makes himself into two; he has within him his other self as the hearer, and the outside audience is merely an extension of this other self of his. The lover seeks his own other self in his beloved. It is the joy that creates the inspiration, in order to realise through obstacles the union.

* * * * *

The singer is translating his song into singing, his joy into forms, and the hearer has to translate back the singing into the original joy; then the communion between the singer and the hearer is complete. The infinite joy is manifesting itself in manifold forms, taking upon itself the bondage of law, and we fulfil our destiny when we go back from forms to joy, from law to the love, when we untie the knot of the finite and hark back to the infinite.

—*Ibid.*, pp. 86-87.

Tagore believes in the Buddhist religious philosophy of joy. He considers joy as the most ideal and important component of *Brahma-vihara,* the Infinite Love. The journey from law to love and vice versa by means of joy is exciting because in both cases there are exercises of love, sacrifice, devotion and humility which carry forth the vision of every religion par excellence. Tagore goes a step further with unison of joy and religion in the same sense that he places love as the supreme element of consciousness for all and thereby makes an infinite endeavour to be one with *Sarvanubhu,* the All Feeler. This is why he wants us to learn the lesson of joy from the sky with love:

> Want of love is a degree of callousness; for love is the perfection of consciousness. We do not love because we do not comprehend, or rather we do not comprehend because we do not love. For love is the ultimate meaning of everything around us. It is not a mere sentiment; it is truth; it is the joy that is at the root of all creation. It is the white light of pure consciousness that emanates from Brahma. So, to be one with this *sarvanubhu*, this all-feeling being who is in the external sky, as well as in our inner soul, we must attain to that summit of consciousness, which is love: *Who could have breathed or moved if the sky were not filled with joy, with love?*[6] It is through the heightening of our consciousness into love, and extending it all over the world, that we can attain *Brahma-vihara,* communion with this infinite joy.
>
> —*Ibid.*, pp. 88-89.

The quest for the Eternal Man as Tagore makes in his quest for joy is the unending search for beauty which he admits as the blessing of the All Serene. He submits his own yearning for joining the joyous festival of Light:

The touch of joy in the heart of light I receive
Know I that my soul no difference does conceive.
From an ancient lustrous source
In the holy current of conscious course
Initiated have I been
On the forehead, the mark of victory was given.
It has informed that the source of nectar I know
With the Great I can I unite and glow
In this world of wonder
In the avenue of joy I may enter.

—Rabindranath Tagore: *Arogya* ("Convalescence"), *Rabindra-Rachanavali,* Government of West Bengal, Calcutta, 1980, Vol. III, p. 839.

[Translated by me]

Tagore envisions joy as Light Eternal, the light that unites one with the All Joy. This joy breathes an air of fullness, a merge into the infinite for which he makes the soulful prayer:

Let the cocoon of this life unmask
The bright halo of consciousness,
Express the eternal form of truth
By piercing the mist
Let the light of joy of a Man Eternal
Amid all men
Be kindled in my mind.
Beyond the silent world of worldly grievance

Let me behold the blessed form of the Eternal.
Whatever is amply meaningless and crucial in this life,
Whatever embodies falsehood in sham values of the society
Leaving aside all beggarly
And troubled crowd,
Let me know the true meaning with my vivid eyes
Prior to crossing the bar

—*Ibid.*, p. 840.

[Translated by me]

Even in celebrating the mystic and transcendental poignancy of man, Tagore brings joy in the forefront as the light of life—the light that continually seeks the Man of the Heart, *Maner Manush.* This joy is the one of inner vision that calls forth the celebration of fullness. The world of folk songs which Tagore creates in joy welcomes the Man of the Heart not because there is an extrinsic manifestation of joy but essentially because it is a perennial journey for revelation of Truth that abides in and pervades beyond us. In such a quest for joy he designs and adores the nature of a *Baul*—the homeless wanderer—who truly represents the endless striving for unison with the Man of the Heart. As he longs for the journey of the heart:

> The Man of the Heart to the *Baul* is like a divine instrument perfectly tuned. He gives expression to infinite truth in the music of life. And the longing for the truth which is in us, which we have not yet realised, breaks out in the following *Baul* song:

Where shall I meet him, the man of the Heart?
He is lost to me and I seek him wandering from land to land
I am listless for that moonrise of beauty,
Which is to light my life,
Which I long to see in the fullness of vision, in the gladness of heart.

—Rabindranath Tagore: "An Indian Folk Religion", *Creative Unity,* Macmillan & Co. Ltd., London, 1962, pp. 78-79.

To celebrate joy without celebrating and welcoming the Man of the Heart would be to bid farewell to the All Joyful—*Sarvananda.* Tagore, therefore, advises us to call the All Joyful in the breast and the grand unison with the All Joyful would then be possible despite the fact that none knows when the encounter will take place. As he frankly submits:

The Man of the Heart He is, why do you keep Him
Seated beside the door of your eyes;
Why not call Him in your breast, let eyes be
Washed away with the streams of eyes!
When lights will be extinguished and the night will come,
Spread the seat in your heart.
In darkness of separation will He in secret arrive.
In His secret path of arrival and departure
In His own accord will He come and depart.
When you promise to bind Him, He remains not,

The string does remain.
Bind yourself aside with that string alone.

—Rabindranath Tagore: *Gaan, Rabindra-Rachanavali,* Government of West Bengal, Calcutta, 1980, Vol. IV, No. 1392, p. 538.

[Translated by me]

Bereft of light, the world of joy to encounter the All Beautiful still persists. Therefore, Tagore makes a far more inward journey, for the vision of joy has already opened the golden gate of unison with the Lord beyond sorrow and happiness:

When I was bereft of vision
My time was spent in the play of tunes but I found no joy.
Building the walls of the playhouse, I was rapt in whims,
When you came by cracking the fountain, my yoke is over.
The game of happiness I like no more, I have found joy.
O my Terrible, my Fierce, my little slumber is gone,
You've tuned up my rhythm with violent pains anew.
The day when, in the guise of fire, you took away my all,
I became perfect on that day and my conflicts ended.
O joy, I have been in unison with you
Beyond the banks of sorrow and happiness!

—*Ibid.*, No. 1614, p. 615.

[Translated by me]

The world of joy as Tagore visualises is one of religion and fullness. It is a world in which every revelation is one of joy of the deathless. It is a world where joy is spread over the sky and the air, the mind and the heart, anywhere and everywhere. It is a world where there is no dishonour or fame, hatred or ill-feeling. When one enters this world of joy and is rapt in the ceremony of joy, one is above fear and littleness, greed and selfishness. When one embraces joy as ever endearing, one is free from either any conflict or hesitation, loss or pain, coercion or humiliation. Joy not only prepares one to respond to the ceremony of Nature but also to that of the inner world to become restrained, poised, solemn, sombre and serene. Honour and happiness, grandeur and affluence find a new habitation and meaning to one who is humble and dedicated to the All Joyful. The spirit that one receives from such an adherence to the All Joyful is the spirit of finer sensibilities and softer consciousness by means of the ever effulging beauty of sacrifice of the little self and welcome of the Greater I who is happy with the joyful void. Let the mind work up with the stirring music of that Greater I so that the fear of destruction, desolation, disappointment and desire is swept away by the overflowing stream of joy.

Tagore wholeheartedly welcomes everyone to nurture and harbour joy because it is the religion of all religions. It comes closest to one who wants to respond to the Creator in all His creation. It comes closest to the best thoughts, best feelings and best intentions of humankind to be in synchronised vision with the All Joyful. It comes to one in such a state of the mind and the heart where there is no entry for littleness and instead, there is an ever present celebration of vastness. In unfolding the beauty of joy, Tagore poignantly exposes the limitless contributions of the All Joyful and advises us to be thrilling partners of joy as the religion of one's very own:

> Today, at this moment of the morning, what waves of activities have surged up in the newly awakened world in the half global part of the earth. In all these valiant endeavour and vast preparations whatever clusters of happiness and sorrow, adversity and affluence are being swept and foamed in villages, cities and distant palaces—everything is only His wish and His joy. Knowing this alone, listen with your spiritual ears to the music of the noise of all the human habitations of this earth in perfect silence. Then speak heart and soul: in happiness and sorrow it is He whose joy abides, in gain or loss it is He whose joy persists, in life and death it is He whose joy pervades—that *anandam Brahmano vidvan na vibheti kutaschana*—one who knows Brahma by the joy of him is free from all fears.
>
> By forgetting little interest and by eliminating little pride, awaken once your own heart in joy. Then only *anandarupamamritam yadvibhati*[7]—One who is manifesting Himself all around in terms of joy in deathless forms, the worship of that Joyful will be complete. Do not harbour on fear, doubt and poverty in the mind. In joy awake in the morning, engage yourself in joy in day's work. At the end of the day, submit yourself in joy amidst silent and pleasant darkness. There is no need for-going anywhere; nor is there any need to seek anywhere as He is existent everywhere in the form of joy. Learn in that form of joy how to achieve joy. Meditate on how to admit in absolute joy whatever is present before you—

In affluence and adversity, remain in goodness,
Remain in joy amidst all ill-name and humiliation,
In joy remain by pardoning all,
In the fountain of the eternal deathless in drinking the juice of peace.

—Rabindranath Tagore: *"Anandaroop"*, *Dharma* (Religion), *Rabindra-Rachanavali*, Government of West Bengal, Calcutta, 1992, Vol. XIV, p. 647.

[Translated by me]

The striving for joy in absolute dedication as above is the key to open the doors of religion par excellence. It is a striving where the All Joyful becomes one with the worshipper and the journey towards fullness of life becomes thrilling and illuminating. The mind is prepared for affinity with the One. The strings are there awaiting the master to be tuned. Joy serves as the endearing communicator with the All Joyful and the better the tuning of the strings of joy, the better the unison with Him.

In the symphony of life and death, Tagore admires joy as the vehicle of meeting the All Joyful. He is not afraid of death because he believes in the religion of joy that leads him towards the path of fullness. This is why he alone can muse:

Sorrow there is, death is there, the pangs of separation ache
Yet there is peace, yet there is joy, yet the unending awakes

Yet life flows on, the sun and the moon and the stars laugh,
With variegated *ragas* does the spring appear in the garden
Waves erase off and rise,
Flowers wither and bloom,
No decay is there nor no end nor even a bit of poverty—
At the feet of that fullness does the mind pray to be placed.

—Rabindranath Tagore: *Gaan, Rabindra-Rachanavali,* Government of West Bengal, Calcutta, 1987, No. 1544, p. 566.

[Translated by me]

Why not join ourselves with Tagore in the muse of the religion of joy?

References

1. Kurvanneveha karmani jijivishet catyam samah.
2. 'For fear of him the fire doth burn,' etc.
3. 'From Joy are born all created things, ' etc.
4. Yadyat karma prakurvita tadbrahmani samarpayet.
5. *Anandarupammamritam yad vibhati*
6. *Ko hyevanyat kah pranyat yadesha akaca anando na syat*
7. He who manifests Himself in deathless forms which His joy assumes.

4

Religion and Humanism: Tagorean Depth of Vision

Man has the indomitable spirit to usher forth the dawn of a new halo of consciousness. He has wit, wisdom and worth. At the same time, he has anger, annoyance and aggression. He has affluence and pomp. At the same time, he has poverty, sorrow and sadness. What triumphs over all the diverse experiences and attainments of man is that he knows how to strive and strive endlessly to harbour a cadence, a resonance and a depth of vision that calls forth the enviable victory of man. How does man know how to strive and how to come out victorious in the teeth of all constraints? And why does he do so? Is it because he nurses the desires and motives as he thinks and does? Or is there a guiding spirit in him which beckons him to be justified to the eternal values of Truth, Beauty and Goodness?

A humanist par excellence, Tagore orchestrates the man in day-to-day actions and contemplations with the inner spirit of consciousness whereby the men in man and vice versa shine out in unending luminous fulfilment. This spirit enables man how to find out the One in order to have the All. The unity of One with the All is the unity of truth with which man is enriched when the desirable end-in-view of soul consciousness becomes a living reality. It is, then, possible to discover the uniformity of law in nature and as soon as this uniformity is discovered, we can discover ourselves in the spirit of love. This is an essential end-in-view of humanism which Tagore ascribes as the religion of man. Tracing the course of man's day-to-day involvements in connection with the search for the One and, therefore, for Truth, he advocates that the harmony of religion and humanism is based on the harmony of man and his surroundings where Love acts as a bliss for mutual understanding and efflorescence:

> Man has every day to solve this problem of enlarging his region and adjusting his burdens. His burdens are many, too numerous for him to carry but he knows that by adopting a system he can lighten the weight of his load. Whenever they feel too complicated and unwieldy, he knows it is because he has not been able to hit upon the system which would have set everything in place and distributed the weight evenly. This search for system is really a search for unity, for synthesis; it is our attempt to harmonise the heterogeneous complexity of outward materials by an inner adjustment. In the search we gradually become aware that to find out the One is to possess the All; that there, indeed, is our last and highest privilege. It is based on the law of that unity which is, if we only know it, our abiding strength. Its living principle is the power that is in truth; the truth of that unity which comprehends multiplicity. Facts are many, but the truth is one.

* * * * *

All our egoistic impulses, our selfish desires, obscure our true vision of the soul. For they only indicate our narrow self. When we are conscious of our soul, we perceive the inner being that transcends our ego and has its deeper affinity with the All.

* * * * *

Man was troubled and he lived in a state of fear so long as he had not discovered the uniformity of law in nature; till then the world was alien to him. The law that he discovered is nothing but the perception of harmony that prevails between reason, which is the soul of man, and the workings of the world. This is the bond of union through which man is related to the world in which he lives, and he feels an exceeding joy when he finds this out, for then he realises himself in his surroundings. To understand anything is to find in it something which is our own, and it is the discovery of ourselves outside us which makes us glad. This relation of understanding is partial, but the relation of love is complete. In love the sense of difference is obliterated and the human soul fulfils its purpose in perfection, transcending the limits of itself and reaching across the threshold of the infinite. Therefore love is the highest bliss that man can attain to, for through it alone he truly knows that he is more than himself, and that he is at one with the All.

—Rabindranath Tagore: "Soul Consciousness", *Sadhana,* Macmillan India Limited, New Delhi, Macmillan Pocket Tagore Edition, 1988, pp. 21-23.

The spirit of unending efflorescence—*Avih*—is the goal of humanism where, as Tagore strongly advocates, the spirit of religion manifests best. We look upon God not in abstraction but in the spirit of humanism and so we worship Him as the eternal source of the highest good, highest enjoyment and highest ascent of the soul. The revelation of God as man is actually the manifestation of the self in perfect goodness and love. This is why Tagore refers to the individual self as the host of the great King of the universe which enjoys freedom and is above the jurisdiction of the King who allows unison with Him in the excellence of love.

Admittedly, Tagore wants emancipation of man lost in the melee of little desires and truth obscured. He emphasises on the revelation of the Infinite in man which is his soul. Tagore elucidates on this point characteristically and highlights the spirit of humanism in a unique pattern:

> Man's cry is to reach his fullest expression. It is this desire for self-expression that leads him to seek wealth and power. But he has to discover that accumulation is not realisation. It is the inner light that reveals him, not outer things. When this light is lighted, then in a moment he knows that Man's highest revelation is God's own revelation in him. And his cry is for this—the manifestation of his soul, which is the manifestation of God in his soul.

Man becomes perfect man, he attains his fullest expression, when his soul realises itself in the Infinite being who is *Avih* whose very essence is expression.

The real misery of man is in the fact that he has not fully come out, that he is self-obscured, lost in the midst of his own desires. He cannot feel himself beyond his personal surroundings, his greater self is blotted out, his truth is unrealised. The prayer that rises up from his whole being is therefore, *Thou, who art the spirit of manifestation, manifest thyself in me.*[1] This longing for the perfect expression of his self is more deeply inherent in man than his hunger and thirst for bodily sustenance, his lust for wealth and distinction. This prayer is not merely one born individually of him; it is in the depth of all things, it is the ceaseless urging in him of the *Avih,* of the spirit of eternal manifestation. The revealment of the infinite in the finite, which is the motive of all creation, is not seen in its perfection in the starry heavens, in the beauty of flowers. It is in the soul of man. For there will seeks its manifestation in will, and freedom turns to win its final prize in the freedom of surrender.

Therefore, it is the self of man which the great King of the universe has not shadowed with his throne—he has left it free. In his physical and mental organism, where man is related with nature, he has to acknowledge the rule of his King, but in his self he is free to

> disown him. There our God must win his entrance. There he comes as a guest, not as a king, and therefore he has to wait till he is invited. It is the man's self from which God has withdrawn his commands, for there he comes to court our love. His armed force, the laws of nature, stand outside its gate, and only beauty, the messenger of his love, finds admission within its precincts.
>
> —*Ibid.,* pp. 33-35.

The emancipation of man as humanism caters to one's very being always awaits nursling and adoration of *Parama Purusha*—the Person Supreme—who is the ideal representative of the religion of man. Tagore steers our attention to that religion where humanism fosters a living aspiration not in evading the consciousness of individual excellence but in enkindling the infinite truth in every individual to exercise love and freedom. Let there be no obscuration of man which, according to Tagore, is utter dissociation from religion. Let the religion of man be that of sincere endeavour where freedom or *mukti* is marked by a genuine involvement in love for one and all. In the words of Tagore:

> Our greed diverts our consciousness to materials away from that supreme value of truth which is the quality of the universal being, the gulf thus created by the receding stream of the soul. We try to replenish with a continuous stream of wealth, which may have the power to fill but not the power to unite and recreate. Therefore, the gap is dangerously concealed under the glittering quicksand and

things, which by their own weight cause a sudden subsidence while we are in the depths of sleep.

The real tragedy, however, does not lie in the risk of our material security but in the obscuration of Man himself in the human world. In the creative activities of his soul Man realises his surroundings as his larger self, instinct with his own life and love. But in his ambition he deforms and defiles it with the callous handling of his voracity. His world of utility, assuming a gigantic proportion, reacts upon his inner nature and hypnotically suggests to him a scheme of the universe which is an abstract system. In such a world there can be no question of *mukti,* the freedom of truth, because it is a solitary fact, a cage with no sky beyond it. In all appearance our world is a closed world of hard facts; it is like a seed with its tough cover. But within this enclosure is working our silent cry of life for *mukti*, even when its possibility is darkly silent. When some huge overgrown temptation trembles into stillness this living aspiration then does civilisation die like a seed that has lost its urging for germination. And this *mukti* is in the truth that dwells in the ideal man.

—Rabindranath Tagore: *The Religion of Man,* George Allen & Unwin Ltd., London, 1951, pp.72-73.

Even when Tagore speaks of Truth, he identifies it with religion in terms of humanism. The *Satyam* as he idealises as the end-in-view of every human endeavour must have its foundation of humanism that characterises the well-being of mankind. A synchronisation of the outer self and the inner or deeper self through exercise of *Satyam* is the best testimony to the religion of man. The cultivation of such Truth or *Satyam* as a religious component extends the horizon of human consciousness and prepares to realise the One not merely within oneself but also as a great transcendental entity. In the words of Tagore:

> We are born conscious of one thing, which is for us the background to our knowledge of all other truths. It is the truth about *myself*, and consists of an inner reality with certain outer manifestations. The manifestation can be proved and measured, but not the inner reality, or that deeper self, which give to the outer manifestations their unity. There have been people to whom the diverse fact about the movements of any conscious or outer self and all this is real, but not the deeper truth within me, which is One. It requires no help from logic for me to realise the *Satyam*, the truth that One exists who not only comprehends all the facts of my life, but who transcends them.
>
> —Rabindranath Tagore: "The Philosophical Approach to Education", L. K. Elmhirst: *Rabindranath Tagore: Pioneer in Education,* Visva-Bharati, 1961, pp. 85-86.

Tagore makes inroads to dynamic humanism where religion and humanism have no barrier in perfect synchronisation to usher forth an ideal religion of man.

As an aspiring image of the All Serene, man must prove his own self as the embodiment of the Divine Self. This can be proved best only when God in man is loved best. This necessitates a devoted and continual striving for man in purifying his knowing, feeling and willing. And as soon as he qualifies himself in fullness of knowing, feeling and willing, and merges himself in man, he also merges in the true vision of the All Serene:

> Man is the image of God. So, like God, man is also endowed with form and formlessness. Form is man's ego while formlessness is his soul. The soul and the ego are as much beyond together and indispensable to each other as the Infinite is related to the finite. Like God, man is also endowed with three natural powers—willing, knowing and feeling. Just as forms of the world are marching to the formless, so the ego of man is meant for the fulfilment of the spirit. This means that man should develop his willing, his knowing and his feeling in such a way that they can assert the glory of a man's spirit. The criterion of the success of the inner powers of man is: whether man's willing, feeling and knowing conform to those of God. When man merges his individual will into the will of God, his knowledge into the knowledge of God and his love into God's love , he is thereby said to have asserted the rights of the spirit in him. At this stage, man feels that what he does is really the fulfilment of God's will through him; he knows then that, like his own self, all selves are related to God. The discovery of integral relationship between God and all selves introduces him to his natural

> relationship with all selves. So love of God on his part develops into love for all selves. For Tagore, God is man's God and the world of God is man's world. so love for humanity is nothing but love for God.
>
> —Siddheswar Bhattacharya: "Religion of a Poet", *The Calcutta Municipal Gazette,* Calcutta, Tagore Birth Centenary Volume, Supplement Issue, Vol. LXXV No. 21, p. 114.

Incomparably sensitive to the image of man as the image of the All Serene, Tagore glorifies religion as the religion of crystallised humanism where catholicity of vision for emancipation of man is the hallmark of true civilisation. The harmony of humanity as he always cherishes is actually the stepping stone of a perfect religious vision where man is bereft of untruth and where he is always on the alert to safeguard humanism and, therefore, religion from flattery, humiliation, fear and belittlement of the self. In his poem *"Ahavan"*, Tagore clarifies this religio-humanistic vision:

> In the aggrieved history throughout the world
> The stormy wind comes groaning in blinding speed,
> And destroys the apex of civilisation
> Cowed down in fear is religion
> And the treasures of meditation from the immortal
> Is crushed at the feet of the demons;
> Come, ye, the young generation, come, ye all,
> Awake in heroic sound the proclamation
> Of the war of emancipation,

Hold, hold aloft the banner of belief
unvanquished.
On the way broken and blood-stained
The inaccessible is to be crossed
Thro' the chariot undaunted,
And the bridge is to be built by hearts.
With the haunting foot-falls of fear,
Adorn, ye, not with humiliation, forget ye not,
Embracing imprisonment through falsehood
and flattery
Belittle not thy providence.
To save thyself,
Sacrifice not the weak at the feet of the strong.

—Rabindranath Tagore: *"Ahavan", Navajatak (The Newborn), Rabindra-Rachanavali,* Government of West Bengal, Calcutta, 1983, Vol.III, pp. 699-700.

[Translated by me]

Initiated in the Upanishadic spirit of the All Serene as *Ya ekah* (Onc) and *Avarna* (sans colour), Tagore upholds the spirit of humanism as the spirit of man enriched with the divine spirit of renunciation and love. Let the whole of mankind be enkindled with the spirit of goodness for all. Let all live in peace and never with ill-feeling. Therein lies the birth of a new humanism blessed with the blessings of the All Serene. As Tagore poignantly observes:

Regrettably we have narrowed down our vision to more material expectations. But even in the West a real concern to raise superior to material interests is now apparent. There I have crossed men in whom the new spirit of renunciation is personified. Those are men who, freed of the petty bonds of nationalism, feel within them the inner oneness of all mankind, and are ready for every sacrifice in working for the fulfilment of the great ideal. I have seen such men in England; they have accepted insult and hurt from the hands of their own people in their struggle to liberate subject races from the tyranny of power. I have seen such renunciation in France, too—there is Romain Rolland, for instance, an outcast among his countrymen. I have also seen this in the minor States of Europe. I have watched the faces of students in Europe, radiant with the hope of world unity, one bearing with patience and courage the blows they must suffer from the dream of the glorious age ahead.

In this propitious dawn, are we alone to harp on the faults of others and base our construction programmes on ill-feelings? In this new dawn, shall we not remember Him, who is One (*Ya ekah),* who is without distinction of colour *(Avarnah)* and who with His multiple power makes true provision for the inherent needs of each and every class *(vahudhasakti yogat varnananekam nihitartha dadhati)?* Shall we not pray to the Giver of wisdom to unite us all in right understanding *(san oh viddhya subhaya samyunaktu)?*

—Rabindranath Tagore: "The Call of Truth", *Towards Universal Man,* Asia Publishing House, Bombay, 1961, pp. 273-274.

The hallmark of humanism is the cultivation of freedom which, according to Tagore, is the soul of religion. As the spirit of freedom incorporates and nurtures the laws of life and growth best, the religion directed towards positive humanism becomes all he more healthy and dynamic. Tagore makes us alert about the consistent dangers of aping the degenerated past ripe in superstitions in the name of religion and warns us against the robbery of the soul in utter insensitiveness to intrinsic self-obstructions:

> By squeezing human beings in the grip of an inelastic system one forcibly holding them fixed, we have ignored the laws of life and growth. We have forced living souls into a permanent passivity, making them incapable of moulding circumstances to their own intrinsic design, and of mastering their own destiny. Borrowing our ideal of life from a dark period of our degeneracy, we have covered up our sensitiveness of soul under the immovable weight of a remote past. We have set up an elaborate ceremonial of cage-worship, and plucked all the feathers from the wings of the living spirit of our people. And for us—with our centuries of degradation and insult, with the amorphousness of our national unity, with our helplessness before the attack of disasters from without and our unreasoning self-obstructions from within—the punishment has been terrible. Our stupefaction has become so absolute that we do not even realise that this persistent misfortune, dogging our steps for ages, cannot be a mere accident of history,

removable only by another accident from outside.

—Rabindranath Tagore: "The Spirit of Freedom", *Creative Unity*, Macmillan India Limited, New Delhi, 1988, pp. 138-139.

How does Tagore himself make a symphony of humanism and religion? How does he remain above his glory and fame as a religio-humanist in the most disinterested manner and embrace all pitfalls as blessings of being more adhered to the All Beautiful? Here is the answer in the muse:

My mind admits not to account for what I did not receive
In the shadow and light of the heart today
On the flute has been played
This world did I love and that reminiscence
To the mind returns time and again
With the southern wind in the endless spirit
Has my own basket filled in,
Tears deep and dense in the core of the heart exist
In the saga of pain turn meditation a success a mist.
Now and the strings were, of course, torn apart,
But who wails for that?
And yet the tune came again and again and that do I remember today.

—Rabindranath Tagore: *"Gaan", Rabindra-Rachanavali,* Government of West Bengal, Calcutta, 1987, Vol. IV, No. 1412, p. 545.

[Translated by me]

Tagore's concept of freedom in the light of religion and humanism finds a newer avenue of effulgence in cultivating the spirit of the Infinite in man. He looks upon man not in terms of psychology alone, where passion dominates over everything, but in terms of the inherent discipline in Nature with all her beckoning of the Infinite which brings forth a realisation that the All Serene is there in man. The wholeness of his existence allows everyone to assess the values of the past and the present in an unbiased mind so much so that the realisation of the universe in terms of the Infinite becomes a fascinating reality. As Tagore significantly asserts:

> Man must realise the wholeness of his existence, his place in the Infinite; he must know that hard as he may strive he can never create his honey within the cells of his hive, for the perennial supply of his life food is outside their walls. He must know that when man shuts himself out from the vitalising and purifying touch of the infinite, and falls back upon himself for his sustenance and his healing, then he goads himself into madness, tears himself into shreds, and eats his own substance. Deprived of the background of the whole, his poverty loses its one great quality, which is simplicity, and becomes squalid and shamefaced. His wealth is no longer magnanimous; it grows merely extravagant. His appetites do not minister to his life, keeping to the limits of their purpose; they become an end in themselves and set fire to his life and play the fiddle in the lurid light of the conflagration. Then it is that in our self-expression we try to startle and not to attract;

> in art we strive for originality and lose sight of the truth which is old and yet ever new; in literature we miss the complete view of man which is simple and yet great. Man appears instead as a psychological problem, or as the embodiment of a passion that is intense because abnormal, being exhibited in the glare of a fiercely emphatic artificial light. When man's consciousness is restricted only to the immediate vicinity of his human self, the deeper roots of his nature do not find their permanent soil, his spirit is ever on the brink of starvation, and in the place of health full strength he substitutes rounds of stimulation. Then it is that man misses his inner perspective and measures his greatness by its bulk and not by its vital link with the infinite, judges his activity by its movement and not by the repose of perfection—the repose which is in the starry heavens, in the ever-flowing rhythmic dance of creation.
>
> —Rabindranath Tagore: "Individual and Universe", *Sadhana,* Macmillan India Limited, New Delhi, Macmillan Pocket Tagore Edition, 1988, pp. 9-10.

To have an extended vision of the true self by overcoming the constraints of the little self is for what humanism stands. Tagore extends this horizon of humanism in the exercise of goodness where pleasure and pain, sorrow and happiness are directed towards the higher plane of merging with the All Good. This merging with the All Good is the religion of all religions. This religion of humanism teaches one how to rise above sorrow, pain, suffering and other constraints of life and directs one to be devoted to the higher ends-in-view of life which glorify humanism through devotion to one's duties and responsibilities towards others thereby towards oneself and vice versa. A holistic view of life as true humanism always accentuates, makes goodness a pattern, an entity and a way of living one's life in perfect tuning with morality and consciousness. It is to see whether humanism of that kind emerged from goodness changes the perspectives of life in a positive and stimulating way towards merging with the All Good. This elevates one from one's narrow self and encourages one to have a feeling of one's greater or superior self which leads one to become impersonal. The human endeavour to become impersonal from being personal and vice versa with the end-in-view of goodness to be persistently cultivated as a religious and humanistic component is the symbol of realisation of one's life in the Infinite which presents one with at least four-fold ascent and excellence in humanism. First, the little is emancipated and the spirit of goodness shines forth with all aura of brilliance. Second, the personal self rises above the domain of impatience, and forbearance qualifies one to be disinterested and impersonal. Third, the bonds of pleasure and pain are replaced by the spirit of joy eternal. Fourth, the unison of the Infinite and the *Karma-yogi* as the *Gita* elucidates, becomes a living and thrilling reality.

A humanist par excellence in the best efflorescence of religion, Tagore makes inroads to humanism in the same pattern as the *Gita* dictates through the actions and contemplations of a *Karma-yogi* and elevates the spirit of goodness in man in perfect discipline and vision. In his own poignant words:

To the man who lives for an idea, for his country, for the good of humanity, life has an extensive meaning, and to that extent pain becomes less important to him. To live the life of goodness is to live the life of all. Pleasure is for one's own self, but goodness is concerned with the happiness of all humanity and for all time. From the point of view of the good, pleasure and pain appear in a different meaning; so much so, that pleasure may be shunned, and pain be courted in its place, and death itself be made welcome as giving a higher value to life. From these higher standpoints of a man's life, the standpoints of the good, pleasure and pain lose their absolute value. Martyrs prove it in history, and we prove it in every day in our life in our little martyrdoms. When we take a pitcherful of water from the sea it has its weight, but when we take a dip into the sea itself a thousand pitchersful of water flow above our head, and we do not feel their weight. We have to carry the pitcher of self with our strength; and so, while on the plane of selfishness pleasure and pain have their full weight, on the moral plane they are so much lightened that the man who has reached it appears to us almost superhuman in his patience under crushing trials, and his forbearance in the face of malignant persecution.

To live in perfect goodness is to realise one's life in the infinite. This is the most comprehensive view of life which we can have

> by our inherent power of the moral lesson of the wholeness of life. And the teaching of Buddha is to cultivate this moral power to the highest extent, to know that our field of activities is not bound to the plane of our narrow self. This is the vision of the heavenly Kingdom of Christ. When we attain to that universal life, which is the moral life, we become freed from bonds of pleasure and pain, and the place vacated by our self becomes filled with an unspeakable joy which springs from measureless love. In this state the soul's activity is all the more heightened, only its motive power is not from desires, but in its own joy.
>
> —*Ibid.*, pp. 47-48.

Sa no buddhya subhaya samyunaktu—May He grant us the beneficent mind—is the key to Tagore's religion of humanism. A beneficent mind never allows ill-feeling and hatred. Instead, sympathy and love adorn such a mind which is always stimulated by the well-being of others and is never blinded by self-interest which harbours hatred. The inherent want of our self—*nihitartha*—happily endears the want of others—*svartha*—so that our unison with the All Joyful becomes a prized reality. Goodness and joy thus find a living manifestation of knowledge, power and action which are the natural components of humanism.

Tagore directs our attention towards exercise of that form of religion crystallized in humanism where in the words of the Upanishad we feel and translate into reality a happy blending of knowledge, power and action so much so that there is goodness in every action. He beckons us to endear every work as the eternal fountain of joy and goodness and elevates us with his soul-stirring words of prayer to *Visvakarma,* the worker of the universe:

> The Upanishad says: *Knowledge, power and action are of his nature.*[2] It is because this naturalness has not yet been born in us that we tend to divide joy from work. Our day of work is not our day of joy—for that we require a holiday; for, miserable that we are, we cannot find our holiday in our work. The river finds its holiday in its onward flow, the fire in its outburst of flame, the scent of the flower in its permeation of the atmosphere; but in our everyday work there is no such holiday for us. It is because we do not let ourselves go, because we do not give ourselves joyously and entirely up to it, that our work overpowers us.
>
> O giver of thyself! at the vision of thee as joy let our souls flame up to thee as fire, flow on thee as the river, permeate thy being as the fragrance of the flower. Give us strength to love, to love fully, our life in its joys and sorrows, in its gains and losses, in its rise and fall. Let us have strength enough fully to see and hear thy universe and to work with full vigour therein. Let us fully live the life thou hast given us, let us bravely take and bravely give. This is our prayer to thee. Let us once for all dislodge from our minds the feeble fancy that would make out thy joy to be a thing apart from action, thin, formless and unsustained. Wherever the peasant tills the hard earth, there does thy joy

> gush out in the green of the corn, wherever man displaces the entangled forest, smooths the stony ground, and clears for himself a homestead, there does thy joy enfold it in orderliness and peace.
>
> O worker of the universe! We would pray to thee to let the irresistible current of thy universal energy come like the impetuous south wind of spring, let it come rushing over the vast field of the life of man, let it bring the scent of many flowers, the murmurings of many woodlands, let it make sweet and vocal the lifelessness of our dried-up soul-life. Let our newly awakened powers cry out for unlimited fulfilment in leaf and flower and fruit.
>
> —*Ibid.*, pp. 112-114.

A connoisseur of transcendent humanism, Tagore extends and crystallises the horizon of religion in essence and continual evolution of man. He seeks and consolidates the rationale of religion in *Sarvamidam*—all-that-is-ness—where everyone's consciousness of the little self buries all visions of tempering the human whole. Let there be no killing of the human reality in abstraction. Instead, let religion, as Tagore himself admits, make every one of us *pathbhola pathik*—a way-lost traveller in the ascent o humanism.

The search for the All Serene as Tagore himself makes in isolation may appear to be a subject-matter verging on the depth of mysticism. But who ignores his humble submission to the All Serene whose existence is perennial not only in him but in all things and beings?

This is why his words of gratitude discover a new religion of man adoring transcendence in a humanistic fashion:

> I seek Him who lives in my mind.
> As He does exist,
> Stars shine in the sky of my mind at night,
> Flowers bloom in my forest in the morning.
> As He does exist,
> In the light of the stars of the eyes
> There is no such play of beauty and feast of colour
> In endless black and white
> As He remains with me,
> The southern wind awakens my joy in my every limb.
> His message it is that is filled
> In the tune of my song amid an unmindful *taan*
> He swings me in the sweep of sorrow all on a sudden
> He hides Himself amidst work and makes me forget mine.
> As eternal He is to me,
> It is His gladness that at times filled in my moments.
>
> —Rabindranath Tagore: *Gaan, Rabindra-Rachanavali,* Government of West Bengal, Calcutta, 1980, Vol. IV, No. 1097, p. 443.

[Translated by me]

To seek the providence of every person in the feelings and sensitivities of others and vice versa is the benchmark of Tagore's religious humanism. He awaits good sense to prevail over all and even though a romantic outsider often apparently assessed and delicately nurtured with a dubious apprehension that he makes a "hopeless quest"[33] for the religion of man, Tagore is an unparalleled humanistic visionary who never allows any loss of faith in man, which has so long greeted crisis in civilisation and eventually in religion. Tagore is an incomparable humanistic visionary who never allows any loss of faith in man, which has so long greeted crisis in civilisation and eventually in religion. A foreseer of civilisation and, therefore, of humanism, he is always hopeful of the best visions and sensibilities of man who tides over all constraints and shortcomings and nurses a new religion of luminous and challenging humanism. Who ignores his prophetic voice of the new religion of humanism resonant with these soul-stirring words?

> The turning of the wheel of fortune will compel the British one day to give their Indian empire. But what kind of India will they leave behind, what stark misery? When the stream of their two centuries' rule runs dry at last, what a waste of mud and filth will be revealed, bearing a tale of utter futility? There was a time when I used to believe that the springs of a true civilisation would issue out of the heart of Europe. Today, as I am about to quit the world, that faith has gone bankrupt.
>
> I live today in the hope that the Saviour is coming, that he will be born in our midst in this poverty-shamed hovel which is India. I shall wait to hear the message he brings with him, the supreme words of promise he speaks unto man from this eastern horizon to give faith and strength to all who hear.

> I look back to the stretch of past years and see the crumbling ruins of a proud civilisation lying heaped as garbage out of history! And yet I shall not commit the grievous sin of losing faith in Man, accepting his present defeat as final. I shall look forward to a turning in history after the cataclysm is over and the sky is again unburdened and passionless.
>
> —Rabindranath Tagore: "Crisis in Civilisation", *Towards Universal Man,* Asia Publishing House, Bombay, 1961, pp. 358-359.

What, then, is the greatest message of humanism as Tagore endears in his heart of hearts as a true religious visionary? A refreshing and life-endearing humanist, here is his own hint in the words of prayer to the All Serene:

> On many an idle day have I grieved over lost time. But it is never lost, my lord. Thou hast taken every moment of my life in thine own hands.
>
> Hidden in the heart of things thou art nourishing seeds into sprouts, buds into blossoms, and ripening flowers into fruitfulness.
>
> I was tired and sleeping on my idle bed and imagined all work has ceased. In the morning I woke up and found my garden full with wonder of flowers.
>
> -Rabindranath Tagore: *Gitanjali,* Macmillan India Limited, New Delhi, Macmillan Pocket Tagore Edition, 1983, No. LXXXI, p. 54.

Are we prepared to wake up and find our 'garden full with wonder of flowers' in religion and humanism?

References

1. AVIRAVIRMAYEDHI
2. Svavabhiki jnana bala kriya cha.
3. While making an in-depth analysis of Tagore 's religion, Professor Sisirkumar Ghose concludes with the following observation and suggestion:

   Restlessness and vagueness may or may not be beautiful but it justifies the ways of the artist to the world. Tagore's subtle passion for perfection allowed him no permanent peace. To turn this "companion of wayfarers" into a harmless philosopher would be the refinement of folly. To speak of religion, wrote Kaufmann, without disturbing man, is to be a false prophet. Speaking ever of "a homesickness for a faraway horizon of emancipation", Tagore is a subtle but not a false prophet. His religious philosophy is his essay on Living Dangerously. His Religion of Man, the out-reach of man, it is his gamble with destiny and the unborn deity. Perhaps his passion for the ideal self, the–fate-of-each-felt-by-all, will be the saving of our civilization, if it deserves to be saved. Religion at its most romantic, and Rabindrian, is that hunger which no existence, in this or any other world, can ever satisfy. For whatever is or could be the actual, would carry the stigma of thisness or thatness. If the poet's proclamation is not man a boundless finite, whose home and destiny are with Infinitude and only there? Such nympholepsy, passion for the impossible, belongs to a soul of fire rather than to the soil. Here is a country of the mind beyond the mundane. Whether the natural sciences and history can ever be exercised is anybody's guess.

An infinite passion, an eternal pain, the nostalgic cry of the still voice, remains the mark of man the seeker. Till he has found himself, he cannot cease. This is the self-discovery that the poet has done with his solitariness. So long as the fire of that passion burns there will be a place in some corner of the soul for the poet's Religion of Man.

A "hopeless quest", the quest of ages, of Rabindranath, will the Beyond and here now ever come together? The romantic Outsider belongs to a wider brotherhood of Wayfarers. Tender, imperative, haunting, here is tomorrow's news today, flashing across the skyline of a poet's soul. Tread softly, for you tread in a poet's dream.

—Sisirkumar Ghose: *Rabindranath Tagore*, Sahitya Akademi, New Delhi, 1986, Pp. 89-90.

5

Religion and Spirituality: Tagorean Essentials of Excellence

Religion is what one is in terms of one's relationship with the All Best within oneself. Rabindranath Tagore explores, signifies, experiments on and appreciates the All Best not in mere relationship but in extending and intensifying that relationship with excellence and ascent. In such an unending endeavour he makes a further quest for the beyonding of the being which illuminates and enriches religion to adore the excellence of man with a beyonding of consciousness. Therefore, the unison between religion and spirituality as he characteristically unfolds becomes all the more genuine and all pervading, stimulating and living.

Admittedly, Tagore makes a natural and spontaneous entry into the world of joy and freedom, creativity and infinite mystery because all religions convey and sustain all these components as the avenues of efflorescence of one's religious and spiritual endeavour. He himself expresses his awe and wonder in the mystery of Nature as the great manifestation of the All Serene whose blessings are always there in the vast universe. Apart from the beckoning of Nature as the unending revelation of the blessings of the All Serene, the sense of inwardness brings forth three essential elements of religion and spirituality viz. goodness, beauty and the infinite call of vastness. A fusion of all these elements prepares one to enter into the domain of deathlessness and voice forth the great saying *Anandarupamamritam yadvibhati.*

The excellence of religion in fusion with spirituality and vice versa as Tagore seeks through his creative activity in particular has its efflorescence in the word of his poetry. The beckoning of Infinity which he has received as a poet looks forward to heralding a religion of novelty that is elegantly wedded to spirituality. In explaining the reasons for his linkage with the beauty of Bengal in *Sonar Tari* (The Golden Boat), he highlights this fusion of religion and spirituality in terms of excellence which he seeks in the spirit of Infinity:

> To ask a poet to explain the specialities in excitement of poetry of a particular nature in a particular period of life is to harass him. How will he know? The inherent mystery of the changes that takes place in the growth of life is not revealed. All the branches of trees do not spread towards the same direction, they move by turning and twisting themselves. Its scientific reason is hidden in the sky, air, light and on earth. If the tree would have thought over it, yet it would not have found berth in the assembly of the ministry of the process of creation. It would not have the right to cast its vote. It only takes everything to be accepted.

This is its duty by nature. The biologist who is seated outside can rather provide a lot of information.

* * * * * *

There is novelty in infinity. Its very beckoning came to me. The mind responded to it, whatever was already hidden in branches, like buds, began to bloom in light. But the writings of *Sonar Tari* (The Golden Boat) are made with a different background. I was roaming on the rivers and in the villages of Bengal at that time. Its novelty is that of dynamic diversity.

* * * * * *

At times, much more of the language and the tune entered the inmost core of my mind in diverse appearances than whatever came visible to me. I was having that reception of continual acquaintance in my heart.

—Rabindranath Tagore: *Sonar Tari* (The Golden Boat), Introduction, *Rabindra-Rachanavali,* Government of West Bengal, Calcutta, 1980, Vol. I, p. 433.

[Translated by me]

Tagore makes the world of religion wide open in the spirit of gladness which is the essence of spirituality. He never isolates religion from man and vice versa or for its cohesion with spirituality because man is the highest embodiment of both religion and spirituality. He expands the horizon of religion in such a harmonisation with spirituality only because he wants to arrive at the truth that humanism and excellence in both indicate how he is true to his self from the point of view of superior consciousness. Therefore, for better efflorescence of religion and spirituality, Tagore emphasises on liberation of the exaggerated self by means of 'supreme freedom of consciousness'. To become 'more than man' is to seek the All in One and vice versa, which demands a certain pattern of involvement in the goodness of humanity. Therein lies the vision of synchronisation between religion and spirituality in the best order of effulgence. Tagore adroitly elucidates this:

> In the Gita we are advised to work disinterestedly, abandoning all lust for the result. Many outsiders conclude from this teaching that the conception of the world as something unreal lies at the root of the so-called disinterestedness preached in India. But the reverse is the truth.
>
> The man who aims at his own aggrandisement underrates everything else. Compared with himself the rest of the world is unreal. Thus in order to be fully conscious of the reality of all, man has to be free himself from the bonds of personal desires. This discipline we have to go through to prepare ourselves for our social duties—for sharing the burdens of our fellow-beings. Every endeavour to attain a larger life requires of man 'to gain by giving away, and not to be greedy'. And thus to expand gradually the consciousness of one's unity with all is the striving of humanity.

The Infinite in India was not a thin nonentity, void of all content. The Rishis of India asserted emphatically, 'To know him in this life is to be true; not to know him in this life is the desolation of death.'[1] How to know him then? 'By realising him in each and all.'[2] Not only in nature, but in the family, in society, and in the state, the more we realise the World-conscious in all, the better for us. Failing to realise this, we turn our faces to destruction.

It fills me with great joy and a high hope for the future of humanity when I realise that there was a time in the remote past when our poet-prophets stood under the lavish sunshine of an Indian sky and greeted the world with the glad recognition of kindred. It was not an anthropomorphic hallucination. It was not seeing man reflected everywhere in grotesquely exaggerated images, and witnessing the human drama acted on a gigantic scale in nature's arena of flitting lights and shadows. On the contrary, it meant crossing the limiting barriers of the individual, to become more than man, to become with the All. It was not a mere play of the imagination, but it was the liberation of consciousness from all the mystifications and exaggerations of the self. These ancient seers felt in the serene depth of their mind that the same energy, which vibrates and passes into the endless forms of the world, manifests itself in our inner being as consciousness; and there is no break in unity. For these seers there was no gap in their luminous vision of perfection. They never acknowledged even death itself as creating a chasm in the field of appearance and disappearance are on the surface like waves on the sea, but life which is permanent knows no decay or diminution.

Everything has sprung from immortal life and is vibrating with life,[3]for *life is immense.*[4]

This is the noble heritage from our forefathers waiting to be claimed by us as our own, this ideal of the supreme freedom of consciousness. It is not merely intellectual or emotional, it has a ethical basis, and it must be translated into action.

—Rabindranath Tagore: "Individual and Universe", *Sadhana*, Macmillan India Limited, New Delhi, Macmillan Pocket Tagore Edition, 1988, pp. 16-18.

For spiritual excellence in the ways of life and action, man, as Tagore advocates, must have the exercise of goodness for all and, in doing so, the wholeness of life demands a continual crystallisation of action and contemplation. The sacrifice of the self which springs from love and goodness is the key to one's spiritual excellence which heightens one's religion from the innate and inherent depth of vision. This is why death, decay or destruction has very little to impress upon one's spiritual ascent and excellence.

Looking at life positively ensures one's religion of the self as the religion of all and vice versa. Tagore advances a step ahead in coordinating and consolidating religion and spirituality from the standpoint of potentiality and accentuation of perfection in the teeth of terrible constraints. This is best revealed in our endeavour at exploring the ideal of truth which is very often misled in our emotional instabilities apparent, hyperactive and/ or immediate. A certain element of consciousness of the whole expands the domain of the religion of truth so much so that the aura of spirituality is effulged only when we do away with all narrowness of vision in the ideal of truth.

To make a positive journey from existence to essence and excellence is to realise religion in terms of spirituality. Tagore makes this an easy and natural journey because he believes and advocates individuality from this positive vision of consciousness. Religion thus endeared in the womb of spirituality makes an access to one's future self beyond his self-consciousness. The freedom of the self to sacrifice brings religion in the brighter perspective and that perspective leads one towards efflorescence of spirituality. Tagore highlights this spirituality as a *dharma* or religion of the highest order where one comes out of the cocoon of one's little self in the exercise of freedom and proves the excellence of one's divine self.

To qualify oneself in the process of being true to religion is to qualify in the process of transcendence where spirituality finds desirable and distinctive exposures. Hence, the importance of the sacrifice of the self for the cause of others like a flower and a lamp freely sacrificing the funds of fragrance and oil respectively can hardly be overestimated.

In the process of transcendence as above, Tagore follows the same path of emancipation as the one that Buddha does in *Nirvana* which stands for the highest efflorescence of love and sacrifice. Why does he prefer this course? The answer is not far to seek, he advocates religion that inspires one to exercise spirituality of that order where negative freedom or 'freedom of self-will' as he appropriately identifies awaits replacement by the freedom of the superior order that leads to goodness and love. Thus the trio of religion, spirituality and aesthetics creates an ideal avenue of man's advancement in unison with the All Serene.

Tagore bases his religion primarily on joy as the latter is the essence of the former in terms of spirituality. *Anandarupamamritam yadvibhati*—the immortal being manifests itself in joy-form. With this vision of joy as the synthesising factor of religion and spirituality, he equates it with love because love and joy, according to him, are one and the same. Unless one is fully devoted and dedicated to the world of love, the world of love remains alien to him. Realisation of love or joy as a distinctive component of spirituality and, therefore, of religion in its purified, heightened and all-endearing form cannot at all be possible unless one is free from sordid, cheap and matter-of-fact desires. The spirit of truth inherent and dormant in oneself awaits efflorescence in love and joy which one should all the time nurture with care and caution.

Looking upon the universe with a view to realising the role of love and joy and thereby appreciating the perfect unison of religion and spirituality is the realisation of the spirit in each one of us. This spirit leads us to realise the large self—the self that is free from death, decay or destruction and blessed with *paramatmam.* A synthesis of religion and spirituality based on 'the wholeness of the world and our oneness with it' as Tagore advocates for exercise of joy and love towards that direction heightens the vision of man born and baptised in the unending spirit of love. Tagore's own elucidation on this point deserves our attention:

> When we look at the world through the veil of our desires we make it small and narrow, and fail to perceive its full truth. Of course it is obvious that the world serves us and fulfils our needs, but our relation to it does not end there. We are bound to it with a deeper and truer bond than that of necessity. Our soul is drawn to it; our love of life is really our wish to continue our relation with this great world. This relation is one of love. We are glad that we are in it; we are attached to it in numberless threads, which extend from the earth to the stars. Man foolishly tries to prove his superiority by imagining his radical separateness from what he calls his physical world, which, in his blind fanaticism, he sometimes goes to the extent of ignoring altogether, holding it as his direst enemy. Yet the more his knowledge progresses, the more it becomes difficult for man to establish his separateness, and all the imaginary boundaries he had set up around himself vanish one after another. Every time we lose some of our badges of absolute distinction by which we conferred upon our humanity the right to hold itself apart from its surroundings, it gives us a shock of humiliation. But we have to submit to this. If we set up our pride on the path of our self-realisation to create divisions and disunion, then it must sooner or later come under the wheels of truth and be ground to dust. No, we

are not burdened with some monstrous superiority, unmeaning in its singular abruptness. It would be utterly degrading for us to live in a world immeasurably less than ourselves in the quality of soul, just as it would be repulsive and degrading to be surrounded and served by a host of slaves, day and night, from birth to the moment of death. On the contrary, the world is our compeer, nay, we are one with it.

Through our progress in science the wholeness of the world and our oneness with it is becoming clearer to our mind. When this perception of the perfection of unity is not merely intellectual, when it opens out our whole being into a luminous consciousness of the all, then it becomes a radiant joy, an overspreading love. Our spirit finds its larger self in the whole world, and is filled with an absolute certainty that it is immortal. It dies a hundred times in its enclosures of self; for separateness is doomed to die, it cannot be made eternal. But it never can die where it is one with the all, for there is its truth, its joy. When a man feels the rhythmic throb of the soul-life of the whole world in his own soul, then is he free. Then he enters into the secret courting that goes on between this beautiful world-bride, veiled with the veil of the many-coloured finiteness, and the *paramatmam,* the bridegroom in his spotless white. Then he knows that he is the partaker of this gorgeous love festival, and he is the honoured guest at

> the feast of immortality. Then he understands the meaning of the seer-poet who sings, 'From love the world is born, by love it is sustained, towards love it moves, and into love it enters.'
>
> —*Ibid.*, pp. 93-94.

To be in perfect unison with the Supreme Lover as Tagore highlights in his vision of spiritual excellence marks a new horizon of soul-consciousness which unfolds the religion of man in its most luminous radiance. The vision of the All Serene as All Love is effulgent in a more intimate kinship with a silent atmosphere of humble submission like a *veena* spreading the message of joy endlessly:

> Make me thy *veena,* hold me, O hold me up
> The strings would tune on in lovely fingers
> With thy hands tender like the lotus, touch my heart
> My heart would murmur in muse in thy ears
> Sometimes in happiness, in sorrow sometimes
> Would cry looking at thee
> Silently would it lie at the feet in forgetfulness
> None knows in what tuning anew would the muse
> March on towards the void
> The message would move towards the shore of the endless.
>
> —Rabindranath Tagore: *Gaan, Rabindra-Rachanavali,* Government of West Bengal, Calcutta, 1987, Vol. IV, p. 189.
>
> [Translated by me]

To be in total fusion with the All Serene in the spirit of love is the discovery of a new form of spirituality which extends and heightens the horizon of religion. Tagore makes religion dynamic and close to the human heart not by dogmas or theories or rituals but by the spirit of the inherent sensibilities in man enkindled with the halo of love as it were to bring forth the finest essence of goodness. The world of joy that he seeks through such a spirit of love is the world of one's own, very much own, to visualise the All Serene in all splendour and brilliance. It is that spirit of love where the spirit of joy endears the finest essence of truth: *tena tyektena bhunjithah*—thou shalt gain by giving away.

Deeply spiritual in his vision of love, Tagore refines his vision of religion in association with Nature who best teaches him how to be in true fusion with his own stoic world of thoughts weaving the cocoon of consciousness amidst diverse sounds. His world of astonishment further accentuates his spiritual vision where Nature shows the avenue of the religion of joy in serenity:

What a sound echoes
Amid consciousness deep and serene
With what a joy
Did the *veena* on my arm splash
On the consciousness deep and serene
Stealing the mind and the heart
And pouring pleasant juice
And with its touch the thoughts stoical!

—*Ibid.*, p. 614.

[Translated by me]

With such an intense spirit of joy, Tagore unfolds a new religion where the Man of the heart comes closest to man seeking endlessly. The spirit of total self-surrender which alone can unite one with the Man of the heart is to be refined in self-devotion and self-dedication. Such a preparation of the self would obviously lead one to encounter the All Serene. Tagore's remarkable clarity of spiritual vision as above is exposed in the marvellous catholicity of vision:

> The Man of the heart He is, why do you keep Him
> Seated beside the door of your eyes;
> Why not call Him in your breast, let eyes be washed away
> With the streams of tears
> When lights will be extinguished and the night will come,
> Spread the seat in your heart
> In darkness of separation would He in secret arrive,
> In His secret path of arrival and departure
> In His own accord will He come and depart.
> When you promise to bind Him, He remains not,
> The string does remain.
> Bind yourself aside with that string alone.
>
> —*Ibid.,* p. 538.
>
> [Translated by me]

How should the spirit of the self be enkindled? How should the mind be in total submission to the All Serene?

Tagore explores the religion par excellence in terms of spirituality in total self-purification by means of self-surrender:

> Please accept me now, O my Lord, accept me
> O please do not refuse me now,
> Remain seizing my heart.
> I do not want again the day lost sans you,
> Let it go to dust.
> Now let me allow to remain awake day and night
> By expanding my life in your light
> With what an aroma and in what a word
> Have I roamed everywhere
> In cities and in fields!
> Tell me now the message of your own
> Hiding your face nearer my heart
> So many stains and so many truancies
> Are yet there in the depth of the mind
> Please do not tell me to go back once more for these,
> Burn these with fire.

—*Ibid.*, p. 312.

[Translated by me]

The essence of religion that Tagore advocates is actually the essence of spirituality, where human love and aspiration are in perfect unison with divine love and longings. In fact, he strongly believes that every human being should strive for that divine spirit awaiting fullest efflorescence. Then alone religion becomes worthy of its inherent spirit of radiance. Then alone life with all its finest endeavour of effulgence in love and joy becomes the vehicle of the spirit of soul consciousness. To transform and transcend the world with the touch of the infinite mystery in every human being thereby to find perfect kinship with the Supreme One is what we seek in perfect religion in its elevation towards spiritual life and beauty and this is what Tagore poignantly reveals in his elucidation of soul consciousness:

> He whose spirit has been made one with God stands before man as the supreme flower of humanity. There man finds in truth what he is; for the *Avih* is revealed to him in the soul of man as the most perfect revelation for him of God; for there we see the union of the supreme will with our will, our love with the love everlasting.
>
> Therefore, in our country he who truly loves God receives such homage from men as would be considered almost sacrilegious in the west. We see in him God's wish fulfilled, the most difficult of all obstacles to his revealment removed, and God's own perfect joy fully blossoming in humanity. Through him we find the whole world of man overspread with a divine homeliness. His life, burning with God's love, makes all our earthly love resplendent. All the intimate associations of our life, all its experience of pleasure and pain, group themselves around this display of the divine love, and from the drama that we witness in him. The touch of an infinite mystery passes over the trivial and the familiar, making it break out into ineffable music. The trees and the stars and the blue hills appear to us as

> symbols aching with a meaning which can never be uttered in words. We seem to watch the Master in the very act of creation of a new world when a man's soul draws her heavy curtain of self outside, when her veil is lifted and she is face to face with her eternal lover.
>
> —Rabindranath Tagore: *Sadhana*, Macmillan India Limited, New Delhi, Macmillan Pocket Tagore Edition, 1988, pp. 35-36.

The spiritual regeneration of man which crystallises religion as Tagore encapsulates in his realisation of the self always sticks to the end-in-view of continual change and growth in our mode of life so that we can rise above the physical self and encounter the All Serene. Just as in every morning the day is reborn, so we will have to make every moment of our little or physical self recycled and purified in the vision of the Supreme Self which is inherent and directs us towards the fathomless sea of eternity.

The spirit of eternity that beckons the divine self as Tagore visualises in his spiritual endeavour finds an in-depth fulfilment serenely expressed through Nature. This is why his religion is the religion of making a living kinship with her from whom he receives the message of the All Serene, and so he prays:

> Unite me with them who tend your cows
> Who play on the flute in your name
> On the stone-built bank, in this melee of chaos
> Why and for what attraction did I come
> What's the call of the forest leaves whose beckoning is through the grass

> The God of my heart does play in the playhouse
> of the heart with all mysteries.
> This is the news that from the mouth of birds
> did I receive.
>
> —Rabindranath Tagore:*Gaan, Rabindra-Rachanavali,* Government of West Bengal, Calcutta, 1987, Vol. IV, p. 373.
>
> [Translated by me]

The world of spirituality that Tagore seeks in his untiring endeavour in transcendence of religion is to be enkindled with the eternal truth of the Upanishad expressed in *nitya 'nityanam* or the permanent in all that is transitory. Therefore, whatever is transitory in this world gets an ascent in the truth of eternity—an ascent in the very vision of the All Serene. His communion with man and Nature is actually a spiritual endeavour where the spirit of transcendence bids farewell to the sensory world and encounters the world beyond which breaks the barriers of the sensory world.[5]

That we should ever become true to ourselves and to everything and everyone in and around us is that religion which, as Tagore serenely visualises, is a definite step towards transcendence in the forms of spirituality. Such a world of spiritual excellence can be achieved only when one rises beyond the levels of getting and non-getting. This is why there is an eternal craving for the Infinite which nourishes religion towards spiritualism. How to realise this infinite being? Tagore gives a very appropriate and poignant suggestion:

> That we cannot absolutely possess the infinite being is not a mere intellectual

proposition. It has to be experienced, and this experience is bliss. The bird, while taking its flight in the sky, experiences at every beat of its wings that the sky is boundless, that its wings can never carry it beyond. Therein lies its joy. In the cage the sky is limited; it may be quite enough for all the purposes of the bird's life, only it is not more than is necessary. The bird cannot rejoice within the limits of the necessary. It must feel that what it has is immeasurably more than it ever can want or comprehend, and then only can it be glad.

Thus our soul must soar in the infinite, and she must feel every moment that in the sense of not being able to come to the end of her attainment is her supreme joy, her final freedom.

Man's abiding happiness is not in getting anything but in giving himself up to what is greater than himself, to ideas which are larger than his individual life, the idea of his country, of humanity, of God. They make it easier for him to part with all that he has, not excepting his life. His existence is miserable and sordid till he finds some great idea which can truly claim his all, which can release him from all attachment to his belongings.

—Rabindranath Tagore: "Realisation of the Infinite", *Sadhana,* Macmillan India Limited, New Delhi, Macmillan Pocket Tagore Edition, 1988, p. 131.

Tagore has his own eternal quest for spirituality in the form of his great introspection and exploration of the infinite. He frantically craves for that religion which would endear him to encounter the All Serene through the latter's blessings of how to love life in the midst of His creation. As he sticks to the promise of upholding such religion in excellence, he longs for a spiritual ascent in volleys of askance directed towards the All Serene:

> If thou dost not give love in life,
> Why have ye filled in the sky at dawn with such music?
> Why is the garland of stars weaved,
> Why is the bed of flowers laid out,
> Why does the southern wind inform the secret words?
> If thou dost give love in life,
> Why does the sky stare thus towards this face?
> Why, then, at times
> My heart floats the mad-like boat on the sea whose shores it knows not?
>
> —Rabindranath Tagore: *Gaan, Rabindra Rachanavali,* Government of West Bengal, Calcutta, 1987, Vol. IV, p. 538.

[Translated by me]

That in all our thoughts and deeds we must be conscious of the infinite is itself a milestone in the ascent of spiritualism. Tagore is more interested in making an ascent as such than in considering religion apart from man with all experiences of emotions and sensibilities awaiting excellence beyond excellence. In a world of crisis in religion and spirituality what prompts him to make a happy blending of the two is to dispel all vicissitudes and sentimentalism, superstitions and narrowness of vision and involve and instil man as the focal point of exercise of both as complementary to each other or rather as a fusion for making a serene encounter with the All Beautiful.

In making such an exercise as above, Tagore pays more importance to excellence in creativity and critical thinking which allow a warm welcome to whatever stands for Truth, Goodness and Beauty and whatever uphold man the unknown but blessed with the blessings of the All Serene: Be thou best in thyself.

Do we earnestly believe?

References

1. *Iha chet avedit atha satyamasti, nachet iha avedit mahati vinashtih*
2. *Bhuteshu bhuteshu vichintya*
3. *Yadidan kincha prana ejati nisritam*
4. *Prano virat*
5. Swami Ranganathananda makes an introspective and thought provoking enquiry into the nature of man from the standpoint of spiritual consciousness and delves deep into the Vedantic and the Buddhist teachings on spiritualism as follows:

   Man begins his life as an individual limited to his own organic system, fully under the control of its genetic constitution; but his education from birth onwards helps him to overcome this limitation little by little. He slowly develops the capacity to dig affections in other people and to make other people dig affections into him. When consciousness achieves this development, it ceases to be an entirely genetically conditioned object, and starts on its long journey of the unfolding of its infinite possibilities as a subject. Education is primarily concerned with the unfolding of these possibilities with their two spiritual dimensions, distinct but not different, namely, the secular and the social, on the one hand, and the trans-secular and the trans-social on the other.

The ancient Upanishads and Buddha classify all development of consciousness levels into two categories, namely, the *loka* and the *lokottara.* These are technical terms with precise meanings in the science of human development. *Loka* means the sensory world, the world revealed by the five senses. At the individuality and personality levels of human development, consciousness functions at the *loka* level, and the development of consciousness is achieved in the context of inter-action with the natural and social environments. At the personality level, however, there is a slight inner penetration as well, resulting outwardly in a more humanized inter-action in the social context. After getting well established at this second stage of the *loka* level, with its rewarding fruits of ethical and moral awareness and sensibilities, consciousness gets the capacity and urge to rise to the *lokottara* level, if it is not made stagnant and uncreative by inadequate philosophies at the *loka* level.

Lokottara means trans-sensory. The word 'transcendental' in English will be its near exact equivalent. The capacity to rise to the *lokottara* level comes from the fulfillment of ethical demands at the *loka* level. That is why we say, in the language of our own religions that ethical and moral basis is necessary to higher spiritual growth. *Sila* or morality is the basis for the higher spiritual development into *Samadhi* and *prajna,* in the words of Vedantic and Buddhist teachings.

Swami Ranganathananda: "The Science of Raising Consciousness to Higher Levels", *Philosophy and Spirituality,* Bharatiya Vidya Bhavan, Bombay, 1984, pp. 475-476.

6

Religion and Creativity: Tagorean Vision of Serenity

The world of creativity is the world of endless wonder and curiosity. Rabindranath Tagore sanctifies this world with the vision of serenity—the vision that always sustains as the religion of man the creative artist. He solemnises this vision with the aesthetic components of Truth, Beauty and Goodness which are also the abiding components of what true religion always incorporates.

Tagore's vision of serenity as manifested in the cohesion of religion and creativity always adores and advocates the creative soul of a man who is endlessly in quest of uniqueness and freedom. He adores the creative sensibilities that call forth the vision of Paradise effulged in the spirit of goodness as the religion of man. How does he want that creativity to be exercised, and what should be the guiding factor? How to nurture the creative soul as the abode of true religion awaiting apposite dissemination? These and a series of other allied inquiries related to religion and creativity necessitate a reshuffling of our utilitarian and parasitic approach to growth and development by adhering to and learning from Nature and the vast creation as the All Serene has presented us and making a thrilling adventure to the unknown and the infinite. In exploring the religion of an artist, Tagore's vision of serenity in terms of creativity is characteristically exposed as follows:

> When the man-made world is less an expression of man's creative soul than a mechanical device for some purpose of power, then it hardens itself, acquiring proficiency at the cost of subtle suggestiveness of living growth. In his creative activities man makes Nature instinct with his own life and love. But with his utilitarian energies he fights Nature, banishes her from her world, deforms and defiles her with the ugliness of his ambitions.
>
> The world of man's own manufacture, with its discordant shrieks and swagger, impresses in him the scheme off a universe which has no touch of the person and therefore no ultimate significance. All the great civilisations that have become extinct must have come to their end through expression of their humanity; through parasitism on a gigantic scale bred by wealth, by man's clinging reliance on material resources, through a scoffing spirit of denial, of negation, robbing us of our means for sustenance in the path of truth.

* * * * * *

I believe that the vision of Paradise is to be seen in the sunlight and the green of the earth, in the beauty of the human face and the wealth

> of human life, even in objects that are seemingly insignificant and unprepossessing. Everywhere in this earth the spirit of Paradise is awake and sending forth its voice. It reaches our inner ear without our knowing it. It turns our harp of life which sends our aspiration in music beyond the finite, not only in prayers and hopes, but also in temples which are flames of fire in stone, in pictures which are dreams made everlasting, in the dance which is ecstatic meditation in the still centre of movement.
>
> —Rabindranath Tagore: *The Religion of an Artist,* Visva-Bharati Book Shop, Calcutta, 1953, pp. 26-27.

The inherent truth of creativity that sensitises religion of serenity is Tagore's forte in the vision of the eternal man. This is the *dharma* which he wants to revive and re-enkindle in the light of great religious teachers' thoughts and teachings on religion. The civilisation of which we are proud is one that adores freedom and accentuates creativity which serves as an inspiring factor in the advance of man from diverse praxes. The Indian religious spirit of *Santam, Sivam* and *Advaitam* welcomes Nature and the vast universe in true conformity with freedom and creativity. Consequently, freedom is not tarnished by material greed and affluence. Instead, a serene vision of the Man Eternal commands and communicates religion in terms of the serenity of creativity. Tagore's exploration into the nature of man in terms of the above deserves re-thinking right now:

> What is evident in this world is the endless procession of moving things; but what is to be

realised is the supreme human Truth by which the human world is permeated.

We must never forget today that a mere movement is not valuable in itself, that it may be sign of a dangerous form of inertia. We must be reminded that a great upheaval of spirit, a universal realisation of the true dignity of man once caused by Buddha's teachings in India, started a movement for centuries which produced illumination of literature, arts, science and numerous efforts of public beneficence. This was a movement whose motive force was not some addition of exceptional accession of knowledge or power or urging of some overwhelming passion. It was an inspiration for freedom, the freedom which enables us to realize *dharma,* the truth of Eternal Man.

* * * * * *

Progress which is not related to an inner *dharma,* but to an attraction, which is external, seeks to satisfy our endless claims. But civilisation, which is an ideal, gives us the abundant power to renounce which is the power that realises the infinite and inspires creation.

—Rabindranath Tagore: *The Religion of Man,* George Allen & Unwin Ltd., London, pp. 154-155.

Creativity, an identification of the nature of the All Serene Himself is the *sine qua non* of individuality, which conforms to the most enviable religion of man. Tagore extends this essence of creativity in every individual as a divine gift which should be caressed, nursed and cultivated in all serenity of purpose. The Great Family of Man with such a culture of creativity encounters the All Serene in poignancy and fullness. This, then, is the religion that is yet to be respected in our society. This, then, is also the religion which signals the victory of man in the cultivation of the invaluable gift of creative consciousness. Tagore draws our attention to this fact very significantly:

> That to create our own world has been the purpose of God, we see when we find that, even as children we had our one and only pleasure in that play where, with trifling materials, we gave expression to our imagination. That is more valuable to us as children than gold or banknotes or anything else. The same thing is true with regard to every human individual. We forget this value of the individual creative power because our minds become obsessed with the artificial value which is made prevalent in society by other people's valuation of a particular manner of living, a particular style of respectability. We force ourselves to accept that imposition and we kill the most precious gift that God has given us, the gift of creation which comes from His own nature.
>
> —Rabindranath Tagore: "The School Master", *The Modern Review, Calcutta, October, 1924,* p. 373.

That Tagore is dead against mere information which kills the cocoons of creativity and thus deprives us from the world of joy which is a gift of the All Joyful is a religion of man yet to be adhered to in right earnest. The fathomless depth of the Infinite in the world of joy as he time and again makes us aware amidst the exercise of creativity is yet to be translated into reality. The religion we adore in creativity as such in unfolding and visualising the world of joy makes life worthy of meaning in our quest for the All Beautiful in the world of learning.

Like a practical psycho-religious visionary, Tagore delves deep into the domain of creativity and analyses the diverse components necessary for appropriate efflorescence of the human mind. In such an in-depth analysis, he probes deep into the sub-conscious mind which contributes a lot to our creative personality. What are the different disciplines that make a happy fusion between one's personality as such and religion? Tagore identifies poetry, music, fine arts and so on which make a very sensitising, intricate and intensive contribution to discover the world of Truth, Beauty and Goodness along with numerous values of life which can hardly be *taught* but can very well be enjoyably *caught*. In his own words:

> Our conscious mind occupies only a superficial layer of life; the sub-conscious mind is almost fathomless in its depth. There the wisdom of countless ages grow up beyond our view. Our sub-conscious mind, where dwells our soul, must also have its adequate media of expression. These media are poetry and music and the arts; here the complete personality of man finds its expression.
>
> —Rabindranath Tagore: "The Centre of Indian Culture", *Towards Universal Man*, Asia Publishing House, Bombay, 1961, p. 225.

Tagore makes a serene blending of religion and creativity in the most precious end-in-view of the fact that they are one and the same. This leads him to arrive at the unique theory of creativity that it is both *ananda* or joy and *amrita* or deathless. To encounter the All Serene in oneself in such a serene vision of creativity is to highlight a new religion which teaches us how to win over natural sorrow, loss, bereavement or pain and look upon the universe as the great gift to be loved as the embodiment of the grandeur of Truth. Tagore's lifelong experience in creativity wedded to religion presents us with this Truth. Here is a living document in the words of poetry:

> In sorrows, bereavements and agonies of life
> A message of the saint has day by day been brighter in my mind—
> The universe manifests itself in the forms of joy and nectar
> Whatever is little thro' opposed evidence
> Does show its easy skill in dwarfing the great
> One who encounters the grandeur of Truth
> Spread over space and time unending
> In the form of the invisible,
> Glorious has his life become in this world.
>
> —Rabindranath Tagore: *Rogasajyay, Rabindra-Rachanavali,* Government of West Bengal, Calcutta, 1983, Vol. III, No. 25, p. 804.
>
> [Translated by me]

The quest for the Eternal Man that Tagore makes in his own world of creativity is embroidered with a serene vision of the religion of love. For this, the earth becomes his heavenly place to encounter the All Love. This has two-fold blessing for him. First, his creativity finds the most positive arena of efflorescence. Second, his vision of the All Beautiful is never tarnished in any change of canvas whatsoever or howsoever made by the creator. As a consequence, he feels with all sublime creativity the existence of the All Serene everywhere:

The most beautiful
Is adorned in the holy morning
Of the bathing of light
The unending formless
With the touchstone of infinite forms
Is creating images of appreciation
Every day
The welcome of the ever new
At the altar of the ever old,
With the unison of the green and blue firmament
The scarf of the earth
In light and shade goes a-weaving.
The heart-beat of the sky
Does throb from leaf to leaf,
The morning's necklace sparkles
From forest to forest,
The countless songs of birds
Go on thanking the goddess of the affluence of life.
The touch of human love
Does bring forth the meaning of nectar in fusion with all,
Turns the dust of the earth pleasant,
And spreads the throne for the Eternal Man everywhere.

—Rabindranath Tagore: *Arogya* (Convalescence), *Rabindra-Rachanavali*, Government of West Bengal, Calcutta, 1983, Vol. III, pp. 821-822.

[Translated by me]

In making a fusion of love and creativity, Tagore presents a new world of youth with flowers unknown. The name of the beloved, too, is unknown. But that affects very little to love and creativity. He introduces us with a new religion where love and creativity leave an eternal testimony to making an endless adventure into the world of All Love:

> To a new country did I come—
> The broken boat sank, to the bank did I come a-floating
> What a unique hope the language of the mind unknown would make me listen
> The web of weal and woe would be woven in coloured thread!
> The resonance of new songs would ring
> With agony anew I would wander in laughter and tears
> The beloved whose name is yet to be known
> Would adore heart with heart with the garland of flowers unknown,
> With the buoyant youth in the early spring
> All thro' the grass bangles would ring,
> The southern wind would dance in the blooming almond creepers
> With restless dishevelled hair!
>
> —Rabindranath Tagore: *Gaan, Rabindra-Rachanavali,* Government of West Bengal, Calcutta, 1987, Vol. V, No. 1639, p. 623.

[Translated by me]

The revelation of a new concept of death bred and nourished in creativity as Tagore himself does in his creative endeavour brings forth a new vista of religion. It is the religion of creating a symphony of past, present and future and marching ahead with the spirit of the Timeless. Admittedly, he explores a new religion in the form of creativity where expression and non-expression are merged in the avenue of timelessness. His own elucidation on this point in the preface to *Prabhatsangeet* is noteworthy:

> Looking within my heart an idea awoke within me that everything good and evil of my every moment, all my experience of joy and sorrow of day-to-day life are taking an endless image of creation ceaselessly. The real nature of that creativity is the eternal ups and downs of these expression and non-expression. Thinking over this, it seemed to me: what, then, is the meaning of death? Somehow the reply was that life retains everything while death leads. I am dying at every moment and through this earth I am marching ahead towards the avenue of life. It is as if the work of sowing is going on within me—the past, present and future are being sown.
>
> —Rabindranath Tagore: *Prabhatsangeet,* Preface, *Rabindra-Rachanavali,* Government of West Bengal, Calcutta, 1980, Vol. I, p. 61.

[Translated by me]

The vision of serenity that Tagore highlights in creativity is the religion of emancipation in the best order and efflorescence. For emancipation as such, he welcomes freedom in the world of creativity bereft of which one cannot but be a victim to passivity and at the same time cannot but be an atheist also. Absence of freedom in creativity is simply an absence of religion where self-obstruction gobbles up the essence of one's individuality. This is terribly dangerous both for an individual and for the masses as well, where stagnancy in creativity leads to irreligion and unavoidable misfortune. Tagore, therefore, beckons us to endear that form of creativity where our living souls well baked in the warmth of freedom show us how to nourish the living soul to convey the spirit of true religion. In this connection, his own interpretation of the spirit of freedom as an invaluable component of furtherance of creativity as a serene manifestation of the religion of man is noteworthy:

> By squeezing human beings in the grip of an inelastic system and forcibly holding them as fixed, we have ignored the laws of life and growth. We have forced living souls into a permanent passivity, making them incapable of moulding circumstances to their own intrinsic design, and of mastering their own destiny. Borrowing our ideal of life from a dark period of our degeneracy, we have covered up our sensitiveness of soul under the immovable weight of remote past. We have set up an elaborate ceremonial of cage-worship, and plucked all the feathers from the wings of the living spirit of our people. And for us—with our centuries of degradation and insult, with the amorphousness of our national unity, with our helplessness before the attack of disasters from without and our unreasoning self-obstructions from within—the punishment has been terrible. Our stupefaction has become so absolute that we do not even realise this persistent misfortune, dogging our steps for

ages, cannot be a mere accident of history, removable only by another accident from outside.

> Unless we have faith in freedom, knowing it to be creative, manfully taking all its risks, not only do we lose the right to claim freedom in politics, but we also lack the power to maintain it with all our strength. For that would be like assigning the service of God to a confirmed atheist.
>
> —Rabindranath Tagore: "The Spirit of Freedom", *Creative Unity,* Macmillan & Company Limited, London, 1962, Pp. 138-140.

The principle of creative unity that Tagore seeks in religion is the principle of the serenity of One who maintains unity of truth inherent in ourselves. The very urge for creativity in oneself sensitises one to be faithful to this unity of truth which is a positive sign of self-consciousness. This has two practical purposes: first, creativity designed and applied for the purpose of revelation of truth does not allow self-consciousness to be dissociated from the world of freedom and joy in oneself, and second, all creative components maintain a natural course of harmony and there is no room for discord in revelation of the sense of One. The religion that Tagore exposes through creativity is always an altruistic one transcending from 'I' to 'Thou', which makes the vision of the All Serene in oneself glorified in humanity. This is the religion which a creative artist disseminates in freedom and joy. As Tagore poignantly observes:

> The fact that we exist has its truth in the fact that everything else does exist, and the "I

am" in me crosses its finitude whenever it deeply realises itself in the "Thou art". This crossing of the limit produces joy, the joy that we have in beauty in love, in greatness, self-forgetting, and in a higher degree, self-sacrifice is our acknowledgement of this, our experience of the infinite. This is the philosophy which explains our joy in all arts, the arts that in their creations intensify the sense of the unity which is the unity of truth we carry within ourselves. The personality in me is a self-conscious principle of a living unity; it at once comprehends and yet transcends all the details of facts that are individually mine, my knowledge, feeling, wish and will, my memory, my hope, my love, my activities, and all my belongings. This personality which has the sense of One in its nature, realises it in things, thoughts and facts made into units. The principle of unity which it contains is more or less perfectly satisfied in a beautiful face or a picture, a poem, a song, a character of a harmony of inter-related ideas or facts and then for it these things become intensely real, and therefore joyful. Its standard of reality, the reality that has its perfect revelation in a perfection of harmony, is hurt when there is a consciousness of discord—because discord is against the fundamental unity which is in its centre.

Rabindranath Tagore: *The Religion of an Artist,* Visva-Bharati Book Shop, Calcutta, 1953, pp. 15-16.

The realisation of creativity in terms of the essential values of life as Tagore identifies in his religion of creativity also welcomes the world of delight. This world assures us how to win over natural happenings of life such as sorrow, loss, death and so on and encourages us to know the One in every one of us. The spirit of delight derived from the spirit of creativity leads us to the spirit of love which Tagore finds in the realm of the surplus. The emancipation of consciousness in creativity is actually the emancipation of the self for a grand encounter with the All Serene. This is why he adores creativity for realisation of the immortal man—*Amritasya putrah.* In his words:

> Our life gains what is called 'value' in those of its aspects which represent eternal humanity in knowledge, in sympathy, in deeds, in character and creative works. And from the beginning of our history we are seeking, often at the cost of everything else, the value of our life and not merely success; in other words, we are trying to realise in ourselves the immortal man so that we may die but not perish. This is the meaning of the utterance of the Upanishad: *Tam vedyam purusham veda, yatha ma vu mrityuh parivyathah*—'Realise the person so that thou mayst not suffer from death.'
>
> —Rabindranath Tagore: *The Religion of Man,* George Allen & Unwin Ltd., London, 1953, pp. 145-146.

The aesthetic odyssey that Tagore launches in creativity makes religion more illuminating than nursing some dogmas or rituals in the name of religion. This makes delight in his world of creativity very natural and serene.

He takes recourse to the path of self-analysis and self-criticism in quest of religion which itself is a quest for creativity in adoring the Infinite. Such self-realisation, even though exclusively personal, bears a deep note of self-enquiry and serenity that finds delight in encountering the All Serene in a unique aroma of effulgence:

> I felt sure that some Being who comprehend me and my world was seeking its best expression in all my experiences. To this Being I was responsible, for the creation in me is His as well as mine.
>
> * * * * * *
>
> I felt that I had found my religion at last, the religion of Man, in which the Infinite became defined in humanity and came close so as to need my love and cooperation.
>
> —*Ibid.*, p. 148.

The culture o one's creative genius in all its completeness is, as Tagore emphasises, the religion which should be nourished with all care and caution. This allows one's self-expression to be exercised unhindered and appreciated as the invaluable gift of the All Serene. Therefore, the living man born of exercising such creativity should be allowed to enjoy freedom to create and freedom to make us living beings and not mere entities in mechanical abstractions.

Tagore wants to orient professionalism from this end-in-view of creativity. He highlights individuality in terms of freedom one exercises to create beauty and advance elasticity in exploring the Infinite. The society thus groomed in creativity bids farewell to mechanised professionalism and enkindles the spirit of the All Serene in an atmosphere of freedom and spontaneity. In exploring the nature of living personalities in the light of the religion of creativity as above, Tagore adroitly elucidates:

> The people, being living personalities, must have their self-expression, and this leads to their distinctive creations. These creations are literature, art, social symbols and ceremonials. They are like different dishes as one common feast. They add richness to our enjoyment and understanding of truth. They are like making the world of man fertile of life and variedly beautiful.
>
> But the nations do not create, they merely produce and destroy. Organisations for production are necessary. But when actuated by greed and hatred, they crowd, away into a corner the living man who creates, then the harmony is lost, and the people's history runs at a breakneck speed towards some final catastrophe.
>
> Humanity, where it is living, is guided by inner ideals; but where it is a dead organisation it becomes impervious to them. its building process is only an external process, and in its response to the moral guidance it has to pass through obstacles that are gross and non-plastic.
>
> Man as a person has his individuality, which is the field where his spirit has its

> freedom to express itself and to grow. The professional man carries a rigid crust around him which has very little variation and hardly any elasticity. This professionalism is the region where men specialise their knowledge and organise their power, mercilessly elbowing each other in their struggle to come to the front. Professionalism is necessary, without doubt; but it must not be allowed to exceed its healthy limits, to assume complete mastery over the personal man, making him narrow and hard, exclusively intent upon pursuit of success at the cost of his faith in ideals.
>
> —Rabindranath Tagore: "The Creative Ideal", *Creative Unity,* Macmillan & Company Limited, London, 1962, p. 36.

To solemnise creativity as religion par excellence, Tagore emphasises mainly on respecting the inner being which opens out the doors of infinite possibilities and makes natural and spontaneous inroads to inner consciousness. He, therefore, eyes creativity as a serene force of individuality where no compromise is made in bartering freedom of thought and expression, self-devotion and self-identity.

When Tagore speaks of creativity in the light of the above as a serene illumination of self-consciousness, he highlights the religion of respecting oneself in being an endless partner to the All Serene. He advocates the heightening of one's Infinite Being by meas of creativity not simply because he is devoted to creative consciousness but also because he feels in his heart of hearts the transcendence of his inner self towards the all-illuminating Divine Self so much so that he declares himself in unequivocal terms: *c'est moi*—here I am.

Tagore's striving for creativity is, therefore, not a passion as it is very often misunderstood but a dedication in abiding terms of serenity and devotion. This is religion of a very superior kind where self-identity through self-askance and self-crystallisation reaches its zenith through the revelation of the creative self: *Amari chetanar range panna halo sabuj.* This, then, is the religion of a rare kind where the beckoning of the All Serene leads the great creative visionary to voice forth the inner vision of love which merges in the beyonding of consciousness:

None feels the mind of the other
Each comes nearer and departs
Why does the smile of endearment
Die down in tears
When the wind wept away
Flowers bloomed not
With hearts wide open why do they lonely wither away in the hours of the evening?
Look at the face, unite eyes with eyes
Cover not the sweet words of the heart in your heart.
The night will bid farewell, no more will we speak
The morning will mourn with the wailings of the heart.

—Rabindranath Tagore: *Gaan, Rabindra-Rachanavali,* Government of West Bengal, Calcutta, 1987, Vol. IV, No. 130, p. 83.

[Translated by me]

Elsewhere, Tagore explores the religion of creativity in terms of love that best expresses serenity in poignancy:

> What a hesitation did you leave in the mind on
> that day in the full-brimmed evening!
> On your departure from the door you turned
> away your thoughtful endurance
> What a world was there in your mind,
> What a smile did you leave behind in the
> corners of your eyes!
> With a trembling heart I think a-sitting,
> In the distant world you remain.
> A young stork is flying in the sky
> The pains within me are its companion
> For once do I aspire to ask you what you did
> not say at the time of farewell:
> Did it remain, O dear, in the pain adorned in
> fragrance of the drenched jasmine!
>
> —*Ibid.,* No. 1696, p. 668.

[Translated by me]

The eternal urge of the creative mind is to encounter the All Serene. The home of the homeless is never a fiction of imagination but a never-to-be-reached and yet the most prized destination for which the creative soul endlessly craves. Tagore endears this religion not simply as a creative artist but with an ever alert and restless 'I' in order to make a perfect fusion between the home of 'I' and the home of the All Serene in the elegant symphony of creativity and the realisation of the Infinite:

> This 'I' of mine toils hard, day and night, for a home which it knows as its own. Alas, there will be no end of its sufferings so long as

> it is not able to call this home thine. Till then it will struggle on, and its heart will ever cry, 'Ferryman, lead me across.' When this home of mine is made thine, that very moment is it taken across, even while its old walls enclose it. This 'I' is restless. It is working for a gain which can never be assimilated with its spirit, which it can never hold and retain. In its efforts to clasp in its own arms that which is for all, it hurts others and is hurt in its turn, and cries, 'Lead me across.' But as soon as it is able to say, 'All my work is thine,' everything remains the same, only it is taken across.
>
> —Rabindranath Tagore: "Realisation of the Infinite", *Sadhana,* Macmillan India Limited, New Delhi, Macmillan Pocket Tagore Edition, 1988, p. 140.

When would we attune ourselves for the eternal prayer in creativity: 'Ferryman, lead me across'?

Reference

1. Admitting that Tagore is romantic par excellence in his vision of creativity and religion, Professor Sisirkumar Ghose makes a probing analysis of the Poet 's religion as follows:

   The observer of his own mind is too wide-awake a child of the times to leave it at that. Instead of opposing, he tries to annex science, especially the theory of evolution. This is his strategy to subsume God, Nature and Man in one continuum. The limits of man 's physical growth, he tells us, have been reached long back. If evolution is to proceed further, it has to be on psychological lines, a voyage inward. But turning theology into anthropology can be tightrope walking. Tagore does not forget to remind us, in a powerful aside, how the modern adoration of the Machine, the genuflection before Technique, has tied us to the law of the inert and the unconscious. The non-human has triumphed over the human, and "everyone in man 's world the Supreme Person is suffering for the killing of the human reality by the imposition of the abstract". Like every romantic, he has his own critique of reason.

Sisirkumar Ghonqse: " A Poet's Religion", Pl. Omit Rabindranath Tagore, Sahitya Akademi, New Delhi, 1986, P. 86.

7

Religion and Mysticism: Tagorean Beyondings

Mysticism, as Rabindranath Tagore advocates, is the meaning of man. He also advocates it as the incomparable world of the void that teaches the lesson of timelessness. This escalates mysticism as the ascent and beyonding of man and qualifies religion in the truest vision of the All Serene within and beyond man.

More often than not, mysticism with all its definitions of an intrinsic effulgence, a look beyond, a consciousness beyond consciousness or at best the science ultimate, the science of all sciences is actually a quest for religion, in religion and by religion for finer beyonding of consciousness.

An incomparable and unparalleled mystic visionary, Tagore unfolds religion in the efflorescence of mysticism primarily for realisation of three ends-in-view. First, a quest for a balanced and sensitised pattern of leading life in fullness of the perfume of poignancy should be the meaning and making of man. Second, the lessons of religion adorned and sophisticated in mysticism would domesticate the already lost man in the light of love, freedom, affection, care, sympathy, cooperation, humility and austerity with all the finer and softer aesthetic and cultural components of life. Third, liable for bringing about a New Age, mysticism cannot but have a dominating role in reorienting religion to provide the modern man with the spirit of returning to the sacred for an endearing encounter with the *Dervish* within.

Very often averted and considered a blurred and somewhat vague and hounded vision, Tagore's religio-mystic quest for union with the sacred and the divine ensures the true assessment of man and society with all finer possibilities and aspirations for unending regeneration. He qualifies religion in the light of mysticism as a voyage for excellence and ascent for man—a voyage promised to alter and sophisticate the bruised and battered know-how with the yet-to-be know-why. A transcendence frail and flapped, mysticism is perhaps the only way to arrive at the goal of our lost affirmation to the All Luminous. Tagore's religio-mystic beckoning further accentuates the modern man with the eternal askance sans any satisfactory answer: *Ke tumi*(Who art thou)?

Essentially a religious visionary right from childhood as a poet and mystic, Tagore admits that his religious life has its growth in the warmth of boundless mystery that has always presented him with the 'depth of feeling'. As such, he has enjoyed and exercised complete religio-mystic freedom of consciousness of the world with a very keen and sensitive mind. How does he enjoy and appreciate his own religio-mystic development? How does he refer to his own religion serenely synchronised with mysticism? Let us listen to his viewpoints:

> My religion is essentially a poet's religion. Its touch comes to me through the same unseen and trackless channels as does the inspiration of my music. My religious life has followed the same mysterious line of growth as has my poetical life. Somehow they are wedded to each other, and through their betrothal has a long period of ceremony, it was kept secret from me. I am not, I hope, boasting when I confess to my gift of poesy, an instrument of expression delicately responsive to the breath that comes from depth of feeling. From my infancy I had the keen sensitiveness which always kept my mind tingling with consciousness of the world around me, natural and human.
>
> I had been pleased with that sense of wonder which gives a child his right of entry into the treasure house of mystery which is in the heart of existence. I neglected my studies because they rudely summoned me away from the world around me, which was my friend and my companion, and when I was thirteen I freed myself from the clutch of an educational system that tried to keep me imprisoned within the stone-walls of lessons.
>
> I had a vague notion as to who or what it was that touched my heart's chords, like the infant which does not know its mother's name, or who or what she is. The feeling which I always had was a deep satisfaction of

personality that flowed into my nature through living channels of communication from all sides.

It was a great thing for me that my consciousness was never dull about the fact of the surrounding world. that the cloud was the cloud, that a flower was a flower, was enough because they directly spoke to me, because I could not be indifferent to them. I still remember thė very moment, one afternoon, when coming back from school, I alighted from the carriage and suddenly saw in the sky, behind the upper terrace of the house, an exuberance of deep, dark rain-clouds lavishing rich, cool shadows on the atmosphere. The marvel of it, the very generosity of its presence, gave me a joy which was freedom, the freedom we feel in the love of our dear friend.

—Rabindranath Tagore: *The Religion of an Artist,* Visva-Bharati Book Shop, Calcutta, 1953, pp. 10-11.

From joy to love and from love to freedom and vice versa is the fountain of mystic vision that springs from religion. Tagore advocates this religion because it widens the horizons of human consciousness and broadens the vision of the Holy Grail. The realisation of the self in others and vice versa awaits this nursling of mystery and awe where one's religion should be to delve deep into the infinite sea of joy and freedom to be in fusion with the All Love. Even in his vision of Visva-Bharati, Tagore in his end-in-view of the study of man from diverse perspectives welcomes the religio-mystic pursuit as the ideal one for the exercise of peace, goodness and oneness in the assembly of global personalities. As he significantly observes:

> Religious sects are formed in every country and every age owing to a diversity of historical causes. There will always be many, who, by tradition and temperament, find special solace in belonging to a particular sect; and also there will be others who think that the finding of such solace can only be allowed as legitimate within the pale of their own. Between such, there needs must be quarrels. Making ample provisions for such inevitable and interminable squabbles, can there be no wide meeting place, where all sects may gather together and forget their differences? Has India, in her religious ideals, no such space for the common light of day and open air for all humanity? The vigour with which the sectarian fanatic will shake his head, makes onc doubt it; the bloodshed which so frequently occurs for such trivial causes makes one doubt it; the cruel and insulting distinctions between man and man which is kept alive under the sanctions of religion, make one doubt it. Still, in spite of all these, when I turn to look back to India's own pure culture—in those ages when it flourished in its truth—I am emboldened to assert that it is there. Our forefathers did spread a single pure white carpet whereon all the world was cordially invited to take its seat in amity and good fellowship. No quarrel could have arisen there; for He, in whose name the invitation went forth, for all time to come, was Santam, Sivam,

> Advaitam—the Peaceful, in the heart of all conflicts; the Good, who is revealed through all losses and sufferings; the One, in all diversities of creation. And in His name was this eternal truth declared in ancient India:
>
> *Atmavat sarvabhuteshu yah pasyati sa pasyati*
>
> He alone sees, who sees all beings in himself.
>
> —Rabindranath Tagore: *The Centre of Indian Culture,* Visva-Bharati, Kolkata, 2001, pp. 43-44.

With the vision of *Santam, Sivam, Advaitam* as a serene religio-mystic end-in-view of human consciousness, ascent and excellence, Tagore advances his philosophy of the beyonding of being for a fusion with the All Serene. For this he idealises love as a very essential component. An endless quest for the Infinite, which is the primary objective of mysticism, becomes the natural vehicle of religion that wins over time present and past. Undeniably, Tagore's mystic adherence to religion prompts to that kind of ascent and excellence which allows one to merge oneself into the consciousness of the beyonding of being:

> It is widely known in India that there are individuals who have the power to attain temporarily the state of *samadhi,* the complete merging of the self in the infinite, a state which is indescribable. While accepting their testimony as true, let us at the same time have faith in the testimony of others who have felt a profound love, which is the intense feeling of

> union, for a Being who comprehends in himself all things that are human in knowledge, will and action. And he is God, who is not merely a sum total of facts, but the goal that lies immensely beyond all that is comprised in the past and the present.
>
> —Rabindranath Tagore: *The Religion of Man,* George Allen & Unwin Ltd., London, 1953, p. 203.

Quite simple and natural, Tagore enters into the world of mysticism not in terms of rigorous *nirvana* but in the aroma of beauty that stands for his religion. He feels quite at ease with his religion that finds a mystic world in Nature and appreciates the world of beauty as the manifestation of the All Serene within:

> The fragrance that trembles before the breast of the flower
> The song that remains in slumber in the light of dawn
> The lustre that dances in beckoning with the autumnal paddy
> And laughs with the gold and green in light
> That fragrance has my frame built
> That song has woven in me this new *maya*
> The lustre has cast shadow upon my eyes
> Who can hold me within?
>
> —Rabindranath Tagore: *"Utsarga"* ("Dedication"), *Rabindra-Rachanavali,* Government of West Bengal, Calcutta, 1980, Vol. II, No. 21, p. 81.

[Translated by me]

Tagore himself creates the world of mystery and exposes his religio-mystic vision in the beyonding of consciousness. This embraces a new religion where the sense of beauty and joy, love and affection finds a new language of religion in mystic serenity and vastness:

My journey is for many years
And towards a great distance
Out I came first
In the first chariot of flight
With planets and stars in curved lines
I painted my foot-prints
On so many mountains and forests
Of human habitations and beyond.

—Rabindranath Tagore: *Geetimalya, Rabindra-Rachanavali,* Government of West Bengal, Calcutta, Vol. III, No. 14, p. 307.

[Translated by me]

Like an introspective visionary, Tagore adores his religion of love in quest of the All Endless that beckons him to encounter beyond the world of sensuality. All romance, love, sentimentalism and passionate intensity of the heart merge in 'the mystery of the heart'—the mystery of the eternal beyonding of being. What appears to be a romantic vision of love and beauty turns out to be a religion of mystic grandeur:

O Beautiful of my mind, come leaving the *veena*
Only with a clasp of your empty hands
Adore my neck—with a touch of your lotus-like hands
Romance springs up with inmost exhilaration
The trembling and restless breast, the watery eyes,

The enamoured limbs crumble down, the heart alone
The edge of the limb flashes out
As if the tie of sensuality will tear apart

* * * * *

Smiling slowly
Looking at me, O mysteriously sweet!
What do you want to tell me, O intoxicated in love
My Endless, what do you want to make me realise?
No words are needed, only wrap up
My whole body and mind with your covering.
Steal me completely with your force.
My all, with breast upon your naked breast
Let me, O dear, listen to the mystery of the heart.

—Rabindranath Tagore: *"Manas Sundari"*, *Sonar Tari*, *Rabindra-Rachanavali*, Government of West Bengal, Calcutta, 1980, Vol. I, pp. 480-484.

[Translated by me]

The mystic sense of awe and wonder that Tagore upholds in his religion makes a happy and serene atmosphere of cordiality with the All Serene. His salutations bear witness to this fact:

Thou hast come in lovely apparel in the evening,
I salute Thee.
Thou hast smiled in my heart of darkness,
I salute Thee.

To this sky humble and silent, beautiful and deep,
I salute Thee.
In this wind gentle and very calm and dense in drowsiness,
I salute Thee.
In this green seat of the tired earth,
I salute Thee.
In this silent chanting speech of the dumb stars,
I salute Thee.
In this secluded inn at the end of work,
I salute Thee.
In this garland of evening flowers with feast of fragrance,
I salute Thee.

—Rabindranath Tagore: *Geetimalya, Rabindra-Rachanavali,* Government of West Bengal, 1980, Vol. II, No. 112, p. 360.

[Translated by me]

With love as the soulful religion of the self, Tagore makes a mystic entry into the world of the All Serene who becomes his partner of love. Love and the lover in such a mystic aroma of efflorescence break all barriers of unison and become the ever illuminating One, the King of all kings:

Thus it is that the joy in me is so full.
Thus it is that thou hast come down to me.
O thou lord of all heavens, where would be thy love if I were not?

Thou hast taken me as thy partner of all this wealth. In my heart is thy endless play of delight. In my life thy will is ever taking shape.

And for this, thou who art the King of kings hast decked thyself in beauty to captivate my heart. And for this thy love loses itself in the love of thy lover, and there art thou seen in the perfect union of two.

—Rabindranath Tagore: *Gitanjali,* Macmillan India Limited, Macmillan Pocket Tagore Edition, 1983, LVI, p. 37.

An intense rapport with the All Serene in his heart of hearts has enabled Tagore to immerse deep into the mystic world where he humbly submits to the religion of self-humility. Such a submission also highlights how the bond of love has endeared him to visualise the Innermost One in all purity of confession:

More, my lord, more
Prize me with punishment, with greater furore.
I remain in seclusion, I run away quite apart,
Exposed have I been, can I any more myself avert?
Take away all whatever I have in store,
Whatsoever do now for my cure.
Let me be the loser or let defeat come at our door
In market-places, stepping and banks as I stay
My time has waned on the laughter alone and play
Let me see how you can for my eyes tears ensure.

—Rabindranath Tagore: *Gaan, Rabindra-Rachanavali,* Government of West Bengal, Calcutta, 1987, Vol. II, No. 661, p. 288.

[Translated by me]

The quest for joy in the sky and the world as Tagore makes, profusely blesses him with the consciousness that signifies the mystic beyonding of his being. He adores it as the religion par excellence because it brings forth eternal dynamism in the wedding of life and death in mystic identity. This, then, is the 'emancipated area of enchantment', a voidless void where his fullness of mystic vision finds remarkable and lasting efflorescence:

Whatever did I expect with earnest eagerness
The clasp of arms around these
When I removed only then
In that emancipated area of enchantment
The consciousness that shines out
With the morning flight
Do I behold the inseparable identity.
Void it is and empty yet it is not
The message of the saint do I then can conceive—
If the sky remained sans pleasure in all measure
The mind and the body would be motionless in the clasping of drabness
Where could there be the difference between one and the other from the point of life
If there was no joy in the sky?

—Rabindranath Tagore: *Rogasajyay, Rabindra-Rachanavali,* Government of West Bengal, Calcutta, 1983, Vol. III, No. 36, pp. 810-811.

[Translated by me]

How does Tagore expose the religion of the voidless void? How does he enlarge the canvas of the mystic beyonding of being? Here is how he unifies himself in Nature and enjoys the warmth of the religion of fullness of life:

> Amidst the blue of the hill and the horizon
> The union between the void and the earth takes place in rhythm and rhyme.
> The golden light of the sun of the early autumn bathes the forest
> In the bunch of yellow flowers the blue bee seeks honey
> Betwixt them do I remain
> And so all around the sky claps in silence.
>
> —Rabindranath Tagore: *Janmadine, Rabindra-Rachanavali,* Government of West Bengal, Calcutta, 1980, Vol. III, No. 14, p. 854.

[Translated by me]

Prior to his farewell to earth, Tagore welcomes Nature with the same mystic vision as above and introduces us with the beckoning of the sky. An aura of poignancy which adorns his mystic vision becomes not only a personal anecdote or self-expression but also carries the message of the religion of the beyonding of consciousness:

> Open the door
> Make the blue firmament unbarred
> Let the curious fragrance of flowers enter my room.
> Let the first sunshine
> Spread over the whole body and in every vein

Through the murmuring leaves
Let me listen to that very message of greetings
That I am alive
Let the morning
Wrap up my mind with its own covering
As it covers new crops and green fields
The silent language
Of love that I have received in my life
Do I hear in this sky and the wind
With the auspicious invocation do I bathe everyday.
The truth of the whole life like a necklace of gems
Do I behold on the breast of the yonder sky.

—Rabindranath Tagore: *Rogasajyay, Rabindra-Rachanavali,* Government of West Bengal, Calcutta, 1983, Vol. III, No. 27, p. 805.

[Translated by me]

To visualise the soul beyond death is to visualise the countenance of the All Serene. Tagore makes his religion really very rich and poignant in the celebration of such visualisation in a mystic depth of disclosure:

Let the fortune of carrying on this life
Touch the forehead with eternal blessings
Like a gift of lustre sans beginning
In newer awakenings at every dawn
As the threshold of this longevity on earth
Let the deep coverings of emaciation
Drop day by day
At the door of the divine

Like the night wedded to slumber
O Sun, manifest your best appearance,
In that divine disclosure
My own soul beyond death do I behold.

—Rabindranath Tagore: *Janmadine, Rabindra-Rachanavali,* Government of West Bengal, Calcutta, 1980, Vol. III, No. 23, p. 862.

[Translated by me]

As an unparalleled mystic visionary, Tagore unfolds and declares a new chapter of consciousness in the rebirth of man in the religion of fullness. He gives a new definition of 'I' within everyone through an expansion of the horizon of consciousness where self-identity gets a new vision of beyonding amidst the passing of the old and advent of the new. Indeed, his rich mystic experience of life reveals a religion quite serene and poised in the odyssey of timelessness:

In this life of mine woven in the thread of my birthdays
Did I visualise myself in the assembly of diverse manifestations.
Once the new year of the breast of the fathomless sea
Did carry me
With the terrible delirium of waves
Where from one horizon to the other
In the vacant sky on the blank firmament
It does deny the shore
On that day did I behold the picture of the world sans diversity
When with the first line of creation

> The sunken future daily traces its own identity
> Towards the sunrise
> Looking unendingly on the curtain of waves
> Enveloped with the mystery of life, I thought
> My life's covering has not yet been opened
> The I complete in myself
> In secret does remain unknown.
> On newer birthdays
> The line drawn by the artist with the stroke of the brush
> Fails to expose within it the last identity of a picture
> Only do I feel
> The vast flood of the unexpressed all around
> Encircles the day and the night.
>
> —*Ibid.,* No. 2, pp. 843-844.

[Translated by me]

Mysticism as Tagore reflects in his religion is the way of return to the roots—a way, indeed, of homecoming. It flashes in the eternity of love. With the religion of love, this spirit of mystic efflorescence opens up the doors of infinite revelations where the sense of loss and gain is merged in the marriage of the finite and the infinite. Tagore's own elucidation on how love becomes an all-pervading mystic force and how it becomes the religion of all religions is very significant:

> When a man feels the rhythmic throb of the soul-life of the whole world in his own soul, then is he free. Then he enters into the secret courting that goes on between this world-bride, veiled with the veil of the many-coloured

finiteness, and the *paramatmam,* the bridegroom, in his spotless white. Then he knows that he is the partaker of this gorgeous love festival, and he is the honoured guest at the feast of immortality. Then he understands the meaning of the seer-poet who sings, 'From love the world is born, by love it is sustained, towards love it moves, and into love it enters.'

In love all the contradictions of existence merge themselves and are lost. Only in love are unity and duality not at variance. Love must be one and two at the same time.

Only love is motion and rest in one. Our heart ever changes its place till it finds love, and then it has its rest. But this rest itself is an intense form of activity where utter quiescence and unceasing energy meet at the same point in love.

In love, loss and gain are harmonised. In its balance-sheet, credit and debit accounts are in the same column, and gifts are added to gains. In this wonderful festival of creation, this great ceremony of self-sacrifice of God, the lover constantly gives himself up to gain himself in love. Indeed, love is what brings together and inseparably connects both the act of abandoning and that of receiving.

In love, at one of its poles you find the personal, and at the other the impersonal. At one you have the positive assertion—Here I am; at the other the equally strong denial—I am

> not. Without this ego what is love? And again, with only this ego how can love be possible?
>
> Bondage and liberation are not antagonistic in love. For love is most free and at the same time most bound. If God were absolutely free there would be no creation. The infinite being has assumed unto himself the mystery of finitude. And in him who is love the finite and the infinite are made one.
>
> —Rabindranath Tagore: "Realisation in Love", *Sadhana,* Macmillan India Limited, New Delhi, Macmillan Pocket Tagore Edition, 1988, pp. 94-95.

The religion of the mystic vision of love which Tagore advocates has the inherent spirit of transcendence from the finite to the infinite. This transcendental spirit is the only one which would show the way to the pilgrimage to eternity. The religion thus pregnant in the spirit of transcendence and mysticism would always be endless askance of emancipation. Tagore presents a living testimony with All Love as his soulful partner:

> Early in the day it was whispered that we should sail in a boat, only thou and I, and never a soul in the world would know of this our pilgrimage to no country and to no end.
>
> In that shoreless ocean, at thy silently listening smiles my song would swell in melodies, free as waves, free from all bondage of words.
>
> Is the time not come yet? Are there works still to do? Lo, the evening has come down upon

the shore and in the fading light the sea birds come flying to their nests.

Who knows when the chains will be off, and the boat, like the last glimmer of sunset, vanish into the night?

—Rabindranath Tagore: *Gitanjali*, Macmillan India Limited, New Delhi, Macmillan Pocket Tagore Edition, 1988, No. XLII, p. 25.

Rich in the mystic experience of love, Tagore directs and diverts our attention to the religion of the unknown and the unheard. It is the religion of silence and endlessness. It conveys the great and poignant truth that love as a mystic component of the growth of the mind bids farewell to pain and pride and heralds the victory of man in the backdrop of reminiscence and oblivion in the sailing of time. In this respect Tagore's mystic vision presents us with a wonderful and serene religion of love:

In what a dense forest did I lose her
In what a backdrop of reminiscence and oblivion of long-lost life
In light and darkness today
Sometimes do I behold her, sometimes not—
What a sea of dreams with the happiness of unison did she come across
Betwixt the existent and the non-existent
My flute plays on with the *raagini* of *chhayanat*
The dancing of shadow of the *vakul* tree is the unison with the fragrance of flowers
I know not what makes the mind mad,
Which dancer's whirling dress-end touches my body.

—Rabindranath Tagore: *Gaan, Rabindra-Rachanavali,* Government of West Bengal, Calcutta, 1987, Vol. IV, No. 1666, p. 631.

[Translated by me]

Elsewhere, the mystic poignancy of love leads to a new vision of calmness of mind and control of passion:

The trap of love is lain all thro' the world
Who knows where one is trapped
All the glory, alas, tears apart
Eyes flow in tears
Only do you want to have in this happy earth
Know ye not how to give yourself.
With the shadow of happiness will you leave unnoticed
Pain will you wilfully adore
When the flute pays on you know not
Pride plies away
In strings does life scramble.

—*Ibid.,* p. 152.

[Translated by me]

To seek the man of the heart in one's heart as Tagore himself does in all earnestness and humility is the religion of a mystic search where the self is in tune with the Divine Self. It is a religion that breaks all barriers of time and marches on and on towards infinity. The sense of mystery brings forth awe and wonder and the mind spreads the web of eternal askance and curiosity in mystic grandeur:

My man of my heart is in the heart
So I behold Him everywhere

In the stars of eyes, in the stream of light
He exists and so He is not lost
Ye, so I see Him anywhere and everywhere
Whenever I feast my eyes
To hear Him I know not where I went
Alas, I heard Him not
Today in my own heart after my return from
door to door
Never, never will you be able to meet Him
O come in a hurry and see in my own breast
In the two eyes of mine.

—*Ibid.*, p. 329.

[Translated by me]

Fully aware of his own shortcomings, Tagore makes no hesitation in frank admission:

You remained hidden in my heart, I could not
see
I looked outside, towards my heart I looked not.
In all my love, in all strokes and hopes
You were beside me, I went not nearby you.
Like my joy you remained in my play
So I lost myself in joy, the days idly spent
In the poignant heart in secret, in my songs of
joy and sorrow
You have given me tunes but I did not sing your
songs.

—*Ibid.*, p. 375.

[Translated by me]

The mystic vision of religion as Tagore experiences and advocates is the vision of humility and total surrender to the All Serene in gradual advancement from the narrow wills and aspirations towards the solemn transcendence of the self. This serves the mystic fulfilment from two dimensions. First, the transcendence so serenely sought becomes a prized possession of the self. Second, the very transcendence of the self becomes oblivious of its own illumination and acts in total self-sacrifice. This is what Tagore identifies as the essence of true *dharma*, the very nature of man in the exercise of freedom of the self. How does he, as a mystic visionary, prepare himself to be justified to the All Serene and to the religion of his self? Here is the exquisite answer:

> I couldn't offer thee all I have, O Lord,
> My shame and awe, grace and disgrace, my thoughts on happiness and sorrow
> A hundred coverings are there amidst these in many a form
> So I roam a-weeping and so I fail to be with thee
> The pangs of my heart thus remain in the heart
> What happiness is there with what I have?
> And with that I go on crying and thinking
> Why do I fail to offer thee when I encounter thee with these
> The world of all of mine shall I offer thee and win thee, my aspirations.
>
> —*Ibid.,* p. 139.

[Translated by me]

The freedom to think of the All Serene makes Tagore visualise himself in terms of the existence of the Man of the heart in his own self. Such a visualisation fills him with an endless mystic joy and brings forth the gladness of the All Serene. As he muses on the religion of mystic fulfilment:

I seek Him alone who lives in my mind
As He does exist
Stars shine in the sky of my mind at night
Flowers bloom in my forest in the morning
As He does exist
In the light of the stars of the eyes
There's so much of play of beauty and feast of colour in endless black and white
As He remains with me
The southern wind awakens joy in my every limb
His message it is that is filled
In the tune of my song amid an unmindful *taan*
He swings me in the sweep of sorrow all on a sudden
He conceals Himself amidst work and makes me forget my work
As eternal He is to me
It is His gladness that at times fills in my moments.

—*Ibid.,* p. 443.

[Translated by me]

The mystic quest for the highest ideal of freedom is to encounter the religion of the self. It is this religion which teaches us how to sacrifice ourselves like a lamp in its perfect illumination. It is this religion which will teach us the best lesson of mystic emancipation. With self-abnegation and love thus exercised in freedom of the self, the All Serene becomes an inseparable partner in the transcendence of the self. Tagore's own elucidation highlights *dharma* in serene mystic effulgence:

> When we know the highest ideal of freedom which a man has, we know his *dharma,* the essence of his nature, the real meaning of his self. At first sight it seems that man counts that as freedom by which he gets unbounded opportunities of self-gratification and self-aggrandisement. But surely this is not borne out by history. Our revelatory men have always been those who have lived the life of self-sacrifice. The higher nature in man always seeks for something which transcends itself and yet is its deepest truth; which claims all its sacrifice, yet makes this sacrifice its own recompense. This is man's *dharma,* man's religion, and man's self is the vessel which is to carry this sacrifice to the altar.
>
> We can look at our self in its two different aspects: the self which displays itself, and the self which transcends itself and thereby reveals its own meaning. To display itself it tries to be big, to stand upon the pedestal of its accumulations, and to retain everything to itself. To reveal itself it gives up everything it has, thus becoming perfect like a flower that has blossomed out from the bud, pouring from its chalice of beauty all its sweetness.
>
> The lamp contains its oil, which it holds securely in its grasp and guards from the least loss. Thus is it separate from all other objects around it and is miserly. But when lighted it

> finds its meaning at once; its relation with all things far and near is established, and it freely sacrifices its fund of oil to feed the flame.
>
> Such a lamp is our self. So long as it hoards its possessions it keeps itself dark, its conduct contradicts its true purpose. When it finds illumination it forgets itself in a moment, holds the light high, and serves it with everything it has; for therein is its revelation.
>
> —Rabindranath Tagore: "The Problem of Self", *Sadhana,* Macmillan India Limited, New Delhi, Macmillan Pocket Tagore Edition, 1988, pp. 62-63.

The yearning for light as Tagore visualises in Nature has a beckoning for him in the religion of love in worship for the All Serene. This leads him to extend his horizon of consciousness in order to be blessed with the mystic beyonding of existence. How does he listen to the language of the endless? How does he expose the religion of the serene self awaiting the grand encounter with the All Enkindled? Let us listen to his incomparable muse:

> My heart was enkindled in the endless sky
> The painful flute played on in the air
> This yearning for light is the world of mine
> Vacantly does it come back in my life again
> With dresses in legion do thou roam about with diverse strategies
> Know I not whom I have garlanded
> What do I visualise today in my life, all the gardens adorn thee

In poignant destruction do thou identify thyself
for the last time by taking all
That finds language in the sky unending

—Rabindranath: *Gaan, Rabindra-Rachanavali,* Government of West Bengal, Calcutta, 1980, Vol. IV, No. 940, p. 387.

[Translated by me]

Why does Tagore adorn such a religion and synthesise it with mystic poignancy? Perhaps he wants to broaden the horizon of religion in the beyonding of man. More perhaps he finds a symphony of love humane and divine. The All Serene is to be encountered in the religion of the transfer and transcendence of love in a sombre pattern of mystic grandeur:

I know in thy love the message of all love mingles
I seek my salvation in it alone at the day's end
The greatest meditation of love is there, all its bonds are loosened.
In thy heart is the sky of the bird of my heart
O dear, know I that in all the streams of my tired days
Become tireless in the bliss of thy dense-deep night.
The touch of the earth in my body has become lively with thy drink—
The very wealth of my dust adores within thee in a new pattern.

—*Ibid.,* No. 1528, p. 585.

[Translated by me]

With such a grand synchronisation between religion and mysticism in the endless light of love, Tagore makes us prepared for a far more majestic show. It is the climax of his mystic glory in meditation and encounter with the All Love to adorn the seat in the inmost shrine of his heart:

> Life of my life, I shall ever try to keep my body pure, knowing that thy living touch is upon all my limbs.
>
> I shall ever try to keep all untruths out from my thoughts, knowing that thou art that truth which has kindled the light of reasoning my mind.
>
> I shall ever try to drive all evils away from my heart and keep my love in flower, knowing that thou hast thy seat in the inmost shrine of my heart.
>
> And it shall be my endeavour to reveal thee in my actions, knowing it is thy power gives me strength to act.
>
> —Rabindranath Tagore: *Gitanjali,* Macmillan India Limited, New Delhi, Macmillan Pocket Tagore Edition, 1988, No. IV, p. 3.

The mystic self-revelation Tagore makes above has its sound basis on his realisation of the most invaluable religion—the religion of love. As this is entirely based on truth, he allows freedom of joy which is serenely entwined in love. This elevates love in the same harmony as one desires in the fusion of the body and the soul. Tagore characteristically elucidates this fusion of love and joy to have the exquisite end-in-view of oneness with All Love:

> Compulsion is not indeed the final appeal to man, but joy is. And joy is everywhere; it is in the earth's green covering of grass; in the blue serenity of the sky; in the reckless exuberance of spring; in the severe abstinence of grey winter; in the living flesh that animates our bodily frame; in the perfect poise of the human figure, noble and upright; in living; in the exercise of all our powers; in the acquisition of knowledge; in fighting evils; in dying for gains we never can share. Joy is there everywhere; it is superfluous, unnecessary; nay, it very often contradicts the most peremptory behests of necessity. It exists to show that the bonds of law can only be explained by love; they are like body and soul. Joy is the realisation of the truth of oneness, the oneness of our soul with the world and of the world-soul with the supreme lover.
>
> —Rabindranath Tagore: "Realisation in Love", *Sadhana*, Macmillan India Limited, New Delhi, Macmillan Pocket Tagore Edition, 1983, pp. 96-97.

To be a mystic visionary like Tagore is to evolve a new religion of consciousness. It is to be modern beyond modernity in the pursuit of religion.

Do we strive?

8

Religion and Society: Tagorean Perspectives

Religion is how it best comprehends the society. It curves its deepest roots in the society not in bare living but in having and being in fullness. Rabindranath Tagore goes a step further in formulating and accentuating religion as an idea, an identity and an emancipation of oneself from becoming to being and from being to beyonding. He extends the vision of society in terms of religion as a realisation of oneself in each and all: *bhuteshu bhuteshu vichintya.*

To endear the goal of human life as calm and peaceful in order to be *yuktamanav* that is to be at one with the All Serene is, as Tagore advocates, to feel the pulse of the society in terms of altruism which makes religion meaningful and purposeful. That religion is not an isolated force but integrated in the very way of life as a human being denotes the emergence of an enlightened and humane society. Tagore steers our direction to that religion to which the idea of a spirited society is inseparably related. As a matter of fact, the realisation of the universe as the manifestation of the Infinite is a long and arduous process of orientation of the self in the society to win over apparent gain of affluence and cultivate the best social habits and culture in order to lead oneself to the supreme achievement in humility for a grand encounter with the All Serene within oneself.

Drawing our attention to the genesis of civilisation and the contribution of the Indian civilisation in particular as an inherent force of religion which the society exercises and enjoys, Tagore significantly observes:

> Civilisation is a kind of mould that each nation is busy making for itself to shape its men and women according to its best ideal. All its institutions, its legislature, its standard of approbation and condemnation, its conscious and unconscious teachings tend toward that object. The modern civilisation of the west, by all its organised effort, is trying to turn out men perfect in physical, intellectual, and moral efficiency. There the vast energies of the nations are employed in extending man's power over his surroundings, and people are combining and straining every faculty to possess and to turn to account all that they can lay their hands upon, to over. Come every obstacle on their path of conquest. They are ever disciplining themselves to fight nature and other races; their armaments are getting more and more stupendous every day; their machines, their appliances, their organisations go on multiplying at an amazing rate. This is a splendid achievement, no doubt, and a wonderful manifestation of man's

> masterfulness, which knows no obstacle and has for its object the supremacy of himself over everything else.
>
> The ancient civilisation of India had its own ideal of perfection towards which its efforts were directed. Its aim was not attaining power, and it neglected to cultivate to the utmost its capacities, and to organise men for defensive and offensive purposes, for co-operation in the acquisition of wealth and for military and political ascendancy. The ideal that India tried to realise led her best men to the isolation of a contemplative life, and the treasures that she gained for mankind by penetrating into the mysteries of reality cost her dear in the sphere of worldly success. Yet, this also was a sublime achievement,—it was a supreme manifestation of that human aspiration which knows no limit, and which has for its object nothing less than the realisation of the Infinite.
>
> —Rabindranath Tagore: "Individual and Universe", *Sadhana*, Macmillan India Limited, New Delhi, Macmillan Pocket Tagore Edition, 1988, pp. 11-12.

An urge for 'spiritual unity of all human beings' as Tagore visualises in his synthesis of religion and society awaits a re-thinking in right earnest. He seeks the service of the modern and enlightened *Brahmins* who would bring about a radical change in the society where cultivation of the spirit of sympathy would be the efflorescence of the true spirit of religion. This will encourage everyone in the society to translate in practice all the essence of spiritual excellence. As he poignantly refers like a foreseer:

> Our modern Brahmins took recourse to the profession of receiving honour sans remuneration. As a consequence, their honour has gradually become verbal in our society. This is not all. To bring about slackness in the dignified work to which the Brahmins were appointed, the cohesion in the society has also been split day by day.
>
> If the society is to be safeguarded in the eastern way, if drastic change of this age-old big society is neither possible nor desirable by means of the European process, then there is an urgent necessity of this real Brahmin community. They would be poor and scholars as well devoted to religion. They would be like an ideal refuge of the ashramic spirit from diverse dimensions as well as gurus or preceptors.
>
> There is no disgrace in dependence or poverty to that society where a group of people knows how to ignore the affluent, hates luxuries, whose manners are pure, devotion to religion firm and who are engaged in selfless pursuit of dissemination of knowledge. A society that makes one duly honourable is alone honoured by one in return.
>
> —Rabindranath Tagore: *"Brahman"*, *Rabindra-Rachanavali,* Government of West Bengal, Calcutta, 1961, Vol. XII, p. 1030.

[Translated by me]

How to exercise religion in the society in right earnest? How to make a harmonious relationship between religion and society? Tagore has a very clear and specific answer. It is love. Love alone brings forth the true spirit of synthesis between religion and society. Rather is it a very vital force for emancipation of the society in the true religious spirit. Tagore significantly observes on this point very categorically:

> Whenever we would know that needs are not the essentials of the human society but love alone is its profound and elite shelter, then, within a moment, we would be free from all shackles. Only then we would cry out: love, ah, what a relief! No more words, then. For love is an entity within myself. It is not that it compels me by giving me a fillip from outside. If love alone is the theory of the human society, then it is certainly my theory. Therefore, I have, within a moment, been promoted to the world of the freedom of joy, being emancipated from the world of necessity by dint of love. It is as if the dream is shattered within the twinkling of eyes.
>
> This, then, is freedom. What then? Then is dependence. As soon as love enjoys emancipation, it becomes busy in fulfilling its strength in that very arena of emancipation. Then it becomes more active than before. Then it becomes a slave to the poor, too, of the world and even serves the wicked and the down-trodden. This is the catastrophe of emancipation.

—Rabindranath Tagore: *Santiniketan, Rabindra-Rachanavali,* Government of West Bengal, Calcutta, 1961, Birth Centenary Edition, Vol. XII, p. 173.

[Translated by me]

Tracing the evolution of man as a social being, Tagore draws our attention to the religion of man to bring together all the finer essence of human sensibilities which direct and guide man to be universal and truly social. As a matter of fact, the vision of a socio-religious world as he encapsulates in his concept of religion welcomes the fellowship of man in efflorescence of all the essential qualities which bear the significant stamp of truth, beauty and goodness. Then, and then only, one can exercise the true spirit of religion as a social being. In this connection, the following viewpoints of Tagore are significant:

> In the primitive age men wandered alone, each in pursuit of their precarious livelihood. Their temper was fierce, their habits predatory, their behaviour unsocial. As on river banks, food became plentiful, communities took form, and civilisations were born. Tilling the alluvial soil, men grew rich crops year after year. They began to see that individuals could gain much more by mutual aid than by trying to deprive one another. With the food problem solved, the social instinct inherent in the nature of man was stimulated. When, at the invitation of the Earth-Mother, men sat down together, their isolated lives found a basis of brotherhood through their common food.

The realisation came that in union there was not advantage alone but also satisfaction. For its sake the individual would accept suffering and even death. The Earth gives us food in such a way that it gladdens our eyes and enraptures our mind. The golden sunlight flung from sky to sky finds a response in the golden harvest from horizon to horizon. This splendour makes man think not only of his meals but of festive rejoicings.

In the storehouse of the Earth there is, above the provision of our hunger, the nectar of joy. Lakshmi, the Goddess of Plenty, is beautiful as well as benign. The fruit tempts us not merely with its nutriment, but with its form, sweetness and fragrance. As the fruits of the Earth are beautiful, so also is the fellowship of man. The food we eat in solitude may have nourishment, but the food that we eat in fellowship has, in addition, loving kindness. In such a feast of hearts the utensils become elegant, the serving decorous, the viands refined.

Dearth cramps the hospitality of man, on which society is founded. That is why villages had to grow on the threshold of the Earth's store of food. It was through his reunions that the immortal in man has expressed itself; his morality, his literature, his music, his art, the variety of his ceremonials. It was through these that he began to be conscious of his own depths, and the ideal of his own perfection becomes manifest to him.

—Rabindranath Tagore: "City and Village", *Towards Universal Man,* Asia Publishing House, Bombay, 1961, pp. 302-303.

Drawing our attention to the terribly ailing society where the religion of finer sense of civilisation is on the verge of extinction, Tagore warns us against material affluence writ large in the society. This is simply an abnormality of human nature in relation to his being truly social whose religion ought to be a religion of austerity, sympathy and fellow-feeling. As a practical socio-religious visionary, Tagore unfolds the trends and tendencies of modern civilisation and directs our attention to some of the glaring facts of irreligion in social ukase:

> Civilisation today cares for a whole population of gluttons. An intemperance, which could safely have been tolerated in a few, has spread its contagion to the multitude. This universal greed, which now infects us all, is the cause of every kind of meanness, of cruelty and of lies in politics and commerce, and vitiates the whole human atmosphere. A civilisation which has attained such an unnatural appetite, must, for its continuing existence, depend upon numberless victims. These are being sought in those parts of the world where human flesh is cheap. In Asia and Africa a bartering goes on through the future hope and happiness of entire peoples is sold for the sake of providing some fastidious fashion with an endless supply of respectable rubbish.

> The consequence of such a material and moral drain is made evident when one studies the condition manifested in the grossness of our cities and the physical and mental anaemia of the villages almost entirely in the world, for cities inevitably have become important. The city represents energy and materials concentrated for the satisfaction of an exaggerated appetite, and this concentration is considered to be a symptom of civilisation. The devouring process of such an abnormality cannot be carried on unless certain parts of the social body conspire and organise to feed upon the whole. This is suicidal; but before a gradual degeneracy ends in death, the disproportionate enlargement of a particular portion looks formidably great. It conceals the starved pillar of the entire body. The illusion of wealth becomes evident because certain portions grew large on their robbery of the whole.
>
> —Rabindranath Tagore: "The Robbery of the Soul", in L. K. Elmhirst: *Poet and Ploughman,* Visva-Bharati, Calcutta, 1975, pp. 34-35.

The religion of man that Tagore advocates is the religion of an evolution of consciousness which guarantees the wholeness of man and society. Such a wholeness admits truth for a fullness of personality in harmony with everyone in the society. An emancipation of man that he earnestly desires in his end-in-view of religion also eliminates the apparent separateness between man and man in the society in the light of truth and, as such, the religion of man assures all avenues of harmony that makes the society living and evolving in the spirit of creative endeavour in every individual. The vision of a society baptised in the religion as Tagore highlights in nursling individuality is enriched with an evolving consciousness of the One always existent in every human soul and guiding the eternal spirit of *c'est moi*—here I am—in every human being in the society:

Admittedly, in making an introspective study of man as a creative spirit, Tagore unfolds the religion of man as the unifying spirit which assures efflorescence of individuality in the wholeness of being in the society and vice versa as an evolving process of consciousness. How to stimulate the individual in the creative spirit of religion for a better balanced society? What should be the essence of man in terms of society and vice versa in unfolding truth as the end-in-view of consciousness of an evolving vision of perfection of harmony? What should be the essential objective of humanity as an effulgence of religion in the context of individuality and social synchronisation? Tagore's adroit elucidation on these vital issues is significant:

> There is a future for the whole which is in it growth, but in order to bring this about, each unit works and dies to make room for the next worker. While the unit has the right to claim the glory of the whole, yet individually it cannot share the entire wealth that occupies a history yet to be completed.
>
> Of all creatures Man has reached that multi-cellular character in a perfect manner, not only in his body but in his personality. For centuries his evolution has been the evolution

of a consciousness that tries to be liberated from the bounds of individual separateness and to comprehend in its relationship a wholeness which may be named Man. This relationship, which has been dimly instinctive, is ever struggling to be fully aware of itself. Physical education sought for efficiency in a perfect communication with the physical world; the evolution of Man's consciousness sought for truth in a perfect harmony with the world of personality.

There are those who will say that the idea of humanity is an abstraction, subjective in character. It must be considered that the concrete objectiveness of this living truth cannot be roved to its own units. They can never see its entireness from outside; for they are one with it. The individual cells of our body have their separate lives; but they never have the opportunity of observing the body as a whole with its past, present and future. If these cells have the power of reasoning (which they may have for aught we know) they have the right to argue that the idea of the body has no objective foundation in fact and though there is a mysterious sense of attraction and mutual influence running through them, these are nothing positively real; the sole reality which is provable is in the isolation of these cells made by gaps that can never be crossed or bridged.

—Rabindranath Tagore: "The Creative Spirit", *The Religion of Man,* George Allen & Unwin Limited, London, 1953, pp. 47-48.

The significance of religious development in terms of society and vice versa is almost entirely dependent on how the diverse avenues of social and religious differences are mobilised in the spirit of inherent unison with a view to arriving at a point of the true vision of life. Tagore advocates an overhauling of the manifold conflicts in man and society with the religion of synchronisation between different issues and conflicts in man and society, which actually represents the spirit of the history of India. As he poignantly observes:

> The only endeavour on the part of India for ever as visualised by me is to establish unity in difference, direct diverse avenues towards the same objectives and understand without doubt the one in the midst of legion as the core of the heart. The differences apparently felt are not to be destroyed but to be in possession of inherent unison.
>
> To visualise this oneness and to make an endeavour for the dissemination of this oneness are very obvious for India. For this very trait on her part, she has remained indifferent for ever to national glory. Those who fail to feel the distant as the most distant heart and the soul cannot consider the attainment of national glory to be the ultimate goal of life. The endeavour to establish oneself above others lies at the root of political achievement. To relate oneself to others and to try to make a synchronisation between the diverse departments and conflicts within oneself point towards religious and social development.

—Rabindranath Tagore: *"Bharatvarsa O Swadesh", Bharatvarser Itihas, Rabindra-Rachanavali,* Government of West Bengal, Calcutta, 1961, Vol. XII, p. 1029.

[Translated by me]

To explore the ideal law of social development is to explore the religion of individuality.[1] The society that cares for such individuality allows perfection of an individual by a growth that develops within the framework of diversities. Tagore hails that religion of diversity where social interests are always prompted by a sense of self-reverence in visualising the All Serene within each and every member in the society. This is why he advocates a new pattern of education of humane and social consciousness where an individual is christened with the spirit of unity in diversity:

> When we received education of the West for the first time, the refrain which we had from that education is: 'No difference is there between man and man. Therefore, we are going to be grown up in such a way as we would be able to eliminate all our points of difference with the new teacher.' Just at that time, closing his books on religion, the teacher said, 'There's so much difference between the East and the West that there's no scope for overcoming that.'
>
> Well, there are differences, and let there differences be. Diversities direct towards keeping good health. As heat and cold are not one and the same at every place, so the wind blows. Let the different ideals of civilisation be

successful from diverse manifestations. Then that would be a means of mutual exchange of education in that uniqueness.

In fact, there are differences in civilisation; that very diversity is one which is desirable to the creator. The success of this diversity lies in mutual understanding with earnestness of enriched knowledge. The education and exercise that bar the doors of entrance to this indicate barbarities. And, for this, injustice and cruelty are created. What are the symptoms of true civilisation? That is civilisation which encompasses: He alone, who remains in all, knows all—*Sa Sarvajnah Sarvamavivesha*—knows all and enters inside all. The ideal which is in enmity with others is not an ideal at all.

—Rabindranath Tagore: *"Samajbhed"* ("Differences in the Society") , *Rabindra-Rachanavali,* Government of West Bengal, Calcutta, 1961, Tagore Centenary Edition, Vol. XII, pp. 1094-1095.

[Translated by me]

To be proud of dynamism in religion and society is to be proud of true advancement. Tagore directs our attention to that advancement of religion and society whereby we can eliminate all sorts of passivity and are really in a very crystallised position of identification of truth and goodness which mark the desirable avenues of advancement of man in terms of religion and society. Delving deep into human constraints of self-assessment, he adroitly observes:

> In spite of exposing the image of the greatness of our country, the constraint in accepting that lies in weakness of our power, we were devoid of a strong and stable possession but our pride was on the increase. A time was there in yore when we amassed all the perversions of our society and religion owing to our rituals and were enclosed with those enclosures. Now it is due to pride alone that we consider it a symptom of strength by admitting all the perversions forcibly. We would not sweep the room nor would we throw any garbage outside; everything as existent anywhere we would endear and consider it a principle of co-operation by injudiciously safeguarding the gems and jewels along with the dust. Such, then, is the plight of affairs that has taken place amongst us. Indeed, it is ignorance. It is passivity that equally valuates everything as existent anywhere and safeguards them. To it, good and evil, error and truth are one and the same.
>
> —Rabindranath Tagore: *"Khrista"* ("The Christ"), *Rabindra-Rachanavali,* Government of West Bengal, Calcutta, 1961, Tagore Birth Centenary Edition, Vol. XI, p. 504.

[Translated by me]

The spirit of austerity which goes a long way in the religion of social advancement has always been more or less ignored in a materialistic and utilitarian modern civilisation. Tagore has always protested against this irreligious tendency of social ukase. He strongly advocates self-identity in terms of the values of simplicity and austerity which essentially contribute to the ascent and excellence of a civilised society. Unless there is a deep devotion to austerity and naturalness backed up by a spirit of spontaneous ingenuity in every member of the society, there is a formidable disaster in embracing artificialities which cut up the genuine urge for making the society feeble with ills of numerous forms of devaluation of values of austerity and creative endeavour and warns the aching civilisation against being a bandwagon to barbarism in doing away with the ideals of simplicity so vital for advancement of humanism. In his own invaluable words:

> I never consider poverty to be great that is ephemeral. But austerity is more valuable than the consuming materials of the affluent. That is real. I am speaking of that austerity which represents an idea of fullness and not merely absence of affluence. When there would be an awakening of that idea, then, within the twinkling of our eyes, much darkness of that mist of materialism would disappear from the firmament of civilisation. As there is the absence of that idea, the things that are of utmost importance to every man are becoming costly and beyond dependence. Music, food, tourism, entertainment, education, administration, law and order—all are very complicated in a civilised country; all have encroached upon a vast room both inside and outside man. Much of this burden is redundant. The strength of an individual, of course, is revealed in the carrying out of this massive burden, but it does not spell out his abilities.

For this reason, God, who is looking at modern civilisation externally, is visualising it like a demon, an unskilled swimmer's attempt to swim. The water sprinkled out of his strokes of legs and hands is whirling and foaming. He even does not know that there is no real need for so much desperation. The difficulty is: the demon is of firm conviction that there is a special value of kicking hands and legs with a terrific speed. When there will be an awakening of the simple truth of fullness in the heart, then, from the walls of the Western drawing room, the Japanese fan, the Chinese utensils, the horns of the deer, the skin of the tiger—the diverse meaninglessness spread all over its corners would vanish like evil visions. From the hats of maidens, dead birds, feathers, artificial flowers, leaves and heaps of garbage would drop down: their over-dealings with dresses and decorations would find their place in the archaeology of barbarism. The five or ten storey buildings standing with their fists raised towards the sky would bend their heads in shame. What with education or with work or with consumerism, to be christened with the ideal of simplicity would be considered by them the true identity of strength and the inherent nature of man will seize the kingdom of the slaves of external one and keep them seated at the legs.

—Rabindranath Tagore: *"Sikshar Herpher"* ("Topsy-turvy in Education"), *Siksha,* Visva-Bharati, 1973, pp. 145-146.

[Translated by me]

The truth of the eternal Man as Tagore seeks and practises in his social thoughts and experimentations reveals a new vision of religion where he idealises man as the embodiment of the divine spirit always making an introspective adventure of how to attain victory in the efflorescence of fullness. Probing deep into the religion of truth as a social manifestation of man, Tagore exposes how man becomes a victim to hypocrisy under social ukase:

> We do not feel slightly ashamed at admitting that it is enough to go on maintaining the external status alone. We do not even hesitate to say that we can do whatever we would practically like to do but there is no harm if we do not admit it publicly. This type of practice in dishonesty is to be accepted by man under trying circumstances. This is because when your reverence has taken a different source, the people of the society do not feel ashamed by taking recourse to dishonest means in case the society stifles the conventions in the same place. As there are very few heroic personalities amongst people, this state of affairs goes on. Therefore, where the punishment for admitting truth in public is intolerably great, one cannot consider it a crime to take recourse to hypocrisy.
>
> —Rabindranath Tagore: *"Sikshavidhi"* ("Principles of Education"), *Siksha,* Visva-Bharati, 1973, p. 126.

[Translated by me]

For the real welfare of the society, Tagore draws our attention to that religion where society welcomes inner discipline. Such discipline makes ample avenues of understanding and appreciating the true meaning and significance of social strength. More often than not, the religion of strength is in coercion, injustice and frenzy writ large in an undisciplined and irreligious society. Tagore forewarns our endeavour at unfolding and practising the religion of strength in the society from different practical perspectives:

> If we are engaged in disseminating the religion of strength in our country now-a-days, even then, is there no possibility of danger in that affair? Is that danger an outcome from that and whom we consider to be our enemies? Do frenzy, injustice and coercion not strike at the root in the disguise of strength? Does genuine weakness in the form of indiscipline not feign forcefulness? What is not strength but a massacre of peace appears as the most formidable one in the pursuit of strength. At present, the signs of its appearance are being visible in our country visible everywhere, but those amongst us who do not in fact trust it, they, too, do not make any endeavour to keep it away by means of unpardonable rigorous discipline and repudiation. If the strength that stands for religion would have been clearly comprehensible to us, then we could not have for a single moment tolerated this ukase.
>
> —Rabindranath Tagore: *"Deshahit"* ("The Welfare of the Country"), *Rabindra-*

Rachanavali, Government of West Bengal, Calcutta, 1961, Tagore Birth Centenary Edition, Vol. XII, p. 919.

[Translated by me]

An ardent admirer and practitioner of the religion of love, greatness, heroism and sincerity, Tagore transcends the spirit of socialism by infusing the religion of self-renunciation and devotion to the welfare of everyone in the society. He draws our attention to the rich social and cultural heritage and tradition of our country and inspires us to follow the valuable fundamentals of socialism that prompt us to practise the religion of social fullness. Then alone we become true partners of progress of the nation. As he characteristically observes:

> Nation is a living entity, a mental matter. Two things contribute to the inner nature of this matter. These two things are, in fact, the same. Of these, one is existent in the past, the other, at present. One is the old treasure of reminiscence of one and all, the other a mutual agreement, desire to live together and to appropriately safeguard the transfer of undivided inheritance. Man does not readily build himself by single-handed endeavour. In the same way, the nation also continues to be manifested in course of endeavour of the long past time, renouncement of the self, and sincerity. We have been, to a great extent, made by our ancestors. The origin of the fundamentals of the national idea lies in heroism, greatness and achievements of the

> past. The same glory of the masses of the past and the same desire of the masses at present to accomplish a great work together—this alone is the source point of framing a community of masses. Our love will be forceful to the extent of our agreement of renunciation and tolerance of sufferings. We love that house which we have built with our own hands and will deliver it to the future generation. In the song of ancient Sparta there is a saying: 'We are what we were, we would be what you are.' This very simple statement is the national ballad of all countries.
>
> —Rabindranath Tagore: *"Atmasakti O Samuha"* ("The power of the Self and Others"), *Ibid.*, p. 677.
>
> [Translated by me]

The swansong of society in terms of religion and vice versa as Tagore advocates is to find out and practise the living spirit of creativity and humanism which adores love and freedom. He also visualises the seedlings of social harmony to be nursed in the religion of vitality as exercised in a system mechanised or otherwise. For a coherent society, the basic principles emanating from the religion of creative and humanistic endeavour as he prescribes should always have an egalitarian approach to life. In his own words:

> When individual communities, who come to dwell in the same neighbourhood, differ from each other in race and culture the first attempts at unity become too obviously

> mechanical in their classified compartments. Some system of adjustment is needed in kinds of society, but in order that a system should be successful it must completely submit itself to the principle of life and become the organ for the vital functions.
>
> The history of India has been the history of the struggle between the constructive spirit of the machine, which seeks the cadence of order and conformity in social organisation, and the creative spirit in man, which seeks freedom and love for its self-expression. We have to watch and see if the latter is still living in India; and also whether the former offers its service and hospitality to life, through which its system can be visualised.
>
> —Rabindranath Tagore: *A Vision of India's History,* Visva-Bharati, 2002, p. 9.

Serenely introspective in religious vision, Tagore extends the canvas of his social philosophy towards realisation of the One in extinction of personality. As a social visionary par excellence, he prefers to switch over from 'I am' to 'Thou art' where the religion of unison is entirely dependent on the excellence of humility, love and self-sacrifice. The vision so vibrant in social harmony is poignant with the religion of One where all the finer socio-aesthetic components of humility find an artistic and living resonance of fullness.

For a celebration of social harmony in the right spirit of religion, Tagore draws our attention to the ancient Indian civilisation, where the important social component of goodness to one and all is always a living image of socialisation of man. There the religion of Hinduism merges with the religion of realising Brahma as the embodiment of goodness. When one is devoted to the goodness of others, one really becomes deeply involved in the religion of socialisation and, therefore, of humanity where every form of religion advocates the spirit of extinction of the self. Tagore makes a very radical and impressive vision of the religion of man in terms of society from the end-in-view of goodness:

> If we re-establish that eternally alive idea of goodness of our ancestors in our hearts as our living component and apply that in every sphere of our society, then we will also be able to attain the vast Hindu civilisation. It is our duty to educate the society and provide with health, food, wealth and money. Therein stands our goodness. Not to visualise it as a business, but it is the only accomplishment not to hope sans virtue and goodness in exchange for that. That is union of action with the Supreme. To continually recall that is Hinduism. Instead of placing the ideal of the self at the centre of human society, to observe it in the midst of the Brahma is in Hinduism. As a consequence, the idea of goodness towards all, from the beast to every human being, is diverged, and to have renunciation of the self with constant practice becomes as easy as breathing. To tie every one of the society from top to bottom with a large selfless string of goodness—this alone is the bigger endeavour than all other attempts from our end. With the string of unity, the unison of religion should be made between the present

> and the past, between one and the other of the Hindu community. This is the only way for us to attain humanity.
>
> —Rabindranath Tagore: *"Bharatvarshiya Samaj"* ("The Indian Society"), *Rabindra-Rachanavali,* Government of West Bengal, Calcutta, 1961, Tagore Birth Centenary Edition, Vol. XII, p. 683.
>
> [Translated by me]

Tagore extends and invigorates the spirit of goodness as an indispensable and succinct component of religion for socialisation with an inherent spirit of the exercise of freedom and love. This spirit of goodness enables one to exercise the religion of realisation of the higher self. The journey from self-hood to soul-hood is a journey of realisation of the self in harmony with fullness, which alone indicates the true nature and end-in-view of religion. This is a journey which Tagore refers to as the journey for attainment of joy in a state of *bodhi.* And this *bodhi* or emergence of love in infinite joy is the right road to religious efflorescence. How to transcend oneself to practise such a religion for the cause of the society? What should be one's special end-in-view of realising religion as a social being? Tagore makes a very comprehensive analysis of the role of the self to be in perfect tune with religion in the society by harmonising freedom from both positive and negative ends which are love and licence respectively:

> We have a greater body which is the social body. Society is an organism, of which we as parts have our individual wishes. We want our

own pleasure and licence. We want to pay less and gain more than anybody else. This causes scramblings and fights. But there is that other wish in us which does its work in the depths of the social being. It is the wish for the welfare of the society. It transcends the limits of the present and the personal. It is on the side of the infinite.

He who is wise tries to harmonise the wishes that seek for self-gratification with the wish for the social good, and only thus can he realise his higher self.

In its finite aspect the self is conscious of its separateness, and there it is ruthless in its attempt to have more distinction than all others. But in its infinite aspect its wish is to gain that harmony which leads to its perfection and not its mere aggrandisement.

The emancipation of our physical nature is in attaining health, of our social being in attaining goodness, and of our self in attaining love. This last is what Buddha describes as extinction—the extinction of selfishness. This is the function of love, and it does not lead to darkness but to illumination. This is the attainment of *bodhi,* or the true awakening; it is the revealing in us of the infinite joy by the light of love.

The passage of our self is through self-hood, which is independent, to its attainment of soul, which is harmonious. This harmony can never be reached through compulsion. So our will, in the history of its growth, must come through independence and rebellion to the ultimate completion. We must have the possibility of the negative form of freedom, which is licence, but we can attain the positive freedom, which is love.

—Rabindranath Tagore: "The Problem of Self", *Sadhana,* Macmillan India Limited, New Delhi, Macmillan Pocket Tagore Edition, 1988, pp. 68-69.

The religion of freedom and love that Tagore wants to disseminate has its deep roots in the society. As a radical social revolutionary, he strongly advocates mass education not merely to evolve what is best in our age-old tradition and culture, but also to highlight a society re-christened with the religion of oneness. This also broadens the canvas of learning where advancement of the society becomes the primary religion of each and every individual. Tagore refers to our great Indian tradition of yore and emphasises on the practising the religion of altruism by following the rich socio-cultural heritage of our country in course of our educational endeavour:

Like the mediaeval era of Europe, education through the *sastras* alone was fundamental. The special pursuit of this education was made in *toles* and *chatuspathis*, but the role of learning was extended throughout the country. There was a continual exchange between specialised knowledge and general knowledge. There was not that antagonistic relationship between the assembly of scholars and unscholarly locality as between an oasis and a desert. There was no part in the country that did not endear the *Ramayana*, the *Mahabharata* and the religious discourses that would regularly spread through diverse channels. Even those theoretical knowledge that were discussed under strenuous perseverance in philosophy were also irrigated in the soils of the minds of the masses all the time. The food for the tree needs to be made liquid so that the tree might take it in all its branches and twigs. In the same way, serious learning in those days have been simplified and disseminated among the minds of the masses. When public work was a part of religion in our country, the arrangements for reservoirs of water at every village were extensive by nature. To quench thirst, arrangements for water were spontaneously made by all together. There was no need for appealing to the spend-thrift personnel of the royal court for water. In the same way, society has disseminated indigenous learning in spontaneity. Otherwise, the whole country would turn into cruelly black barbarities. Learning, then, was not a property to the learned alone. That was a property of the whole society.

—Rabindranath Tagore: *"Sikshar Vikiran"* ("Dissemination of Education"), *Siksha,* Visva-Bharati, 1973, pp. 214-215.

[Translated by me]

Indeed, the religion of man is the religion of the society where religion stands for the realisation of the great truth: *Sada jananang hridaye sannivishtah*—the All Serene always enthrones in the hearts of all. Such a society makes no room for littleness nor is there any room for austerity in embracing the rich dividends of the best in every religion. Tagore welcomes us to that lotus-land of society where we embrace whatever is best in every religion to widen our vision and broaden our approach to fullness, where we harbour joy and love, beauty and goodness, truth and freedom, sympathy and creative consciousness and where we pray to the All Serene: *Ah noh vuddhya subhaya sangyunaktu*—let our wisdom be in unison with auspiciousness.

Are we ready for making such a fusion between religion and society

Reference

1. It is interesting to note in this connection how Sri Aurobindo comes closer to the views and opinions of Tagore on religious and social development and the role of individuality thereto:

   Man's individuality is the distinction, by this he understands the law of his being and development and in the end to go beyond himself. To do this is the destiny of man and the object of his individual and social existence. This is done primarily through the individual man; for this end man has become an individual soul, that the One may find and manifest Himself in each human being. The object of all society should be, therefore, first to provide conditions of life and growth for individual Man, for all men; secondly, to express in the general life of mankind the power, joy and beauty of the Spirit that has been attained. Freedom and harmony express the two necessary principles of variation and oneness, conditions of healthy progression and successful arrival. The individual will arrive at his possible perfection by a growth from within. It cannot be done brutally, heavily, mechanically. The liberty claimed by the human mind for the individual is no mere egoistic challenge and revolt, it is the primary condition for its self-unfoldment. But individual man belongs not only to humanity, but also to his race type, class type, his mental, vital, physical, spiritual type in which he resembles some, differs from others. It is by working through his group that he enriches his society, that is, his nation. The community stands as a mid-term between the individual and humanity, and it has, like the individual, the right to be itself as against any attempt at domination, uniformity or regimentation. This does not mean that it will refuse contact and interchange with the rest of the world.

—Sri Aurobindo: "The Ideal Law of Social Development", *The Human Cycle,* (Abridged), Sri Aurobindo Pathamandir, Calcutta, 1972, Pp. 20-21.

9

Religion and Education: Tagorean Synthesis

Education is always an invaluable asset to religion. It forms an intrinsic part of religion and crystallises religion from all avenues of poignancy and excellence. It enlivens mankind with that spirit of religion where the role of education for erudition is coupled with that of edification. Added to these, education advances the march of religion as an altruistic and communicative component of ascent and richness culled from all enviable ethos and moorings of man.

As an educational thinker and innovator for centuries to come, Rabindranath Tagore regards education as religion itself, for he looks upon the All Serene as embodied in everyone and awaiting His fullest efflorescence in the best possible cultivation of advancement of learning. In his own life he finds an affinity to religion in and through education which he identifies as an ardent vision, a mystery and a restless quest for life. His ever beaming awe and wonder in quest of religion gets an added and thrilling boost in course of pursuit of education for advancement in all directions where religion has always been a permanent end-in-view of life and fulfilment. In fact, all the avenues of realisation of life encompassing love, action, beauty and the Infinite have been converged in his concept and realisation of religion and, as such, religion is education and vice versa in his vision of the fullness of man.

Tagore, therefore, places the individual as an indivisible part of the universe where the Lord of the Universe, the Boundless Vratapati, awaits the advancement of the individual in erudition and edification. He advances a step further in the synthesis of the vision of religion and education in terms of advancement of life in creative and aesthetic endeavour. Elucidating at length this fusion of education and religion as a creative artist, he characteristically observes:

> My religion is essentially a poet's religion. Its touch comes to me through the same unseen and trackless channels as does the inspiration of my music. My religious life has followed the same mysterious line of growth as has my poetical life, somehow they are wedded to each other, and through their betrothal had a long period of ceremony; it was kept secret from me. I am not, I hope, boasting when I confess to my gift of poesy, an instrument of expression delicately responsive to the breath that comes from the depth of feeling. From my infancy I had the keen sensitiveness which always kept my mind tingling with consciousness of the world around me, natural and human.
>
> I had been blessed with that sense of wonder which gives a child his right of entry

> into the treasure house of mystery which is in the heart of existence. I neglected my studies because they rudely summoned me away from the world around me, which was my friend and companion, and when I was thirteen I freed myself from the clutch of an educational system that tried to keep me imprisoned within the stone-walls of lessons.
>
> —Rabindranath Tagore: *The Religion of an Artist,* Visva-Bharati Bookshop, Calcutta, 1953, p. 10.

Fusing religion with education is Tagore's unique forte in educational experimentations. Quite characteristic to his nature, education is neither a rigour nor a rigmarole but a seeing within—a seeing perhaps more than a mere 'seeing into the life of things'. It *is* and *ought to be* freedom—freedom from all bondage of ignorance and narrowness. This is why the harmonious blending of religion and education which he always thought and experimented in his educational endeavour makes inroads to unending inner consciousness of a harmony of human relationship that always ventilates the true spirit of religion. In his own vision of the cohesion between religion and education, he exposes this wide canvas of freedom of knowledge which, in fact, speaks elegantly for freedom of religion in terms of human development:

> Looking back upon those moments of my boyhood days, when my mind seemed to float poised upon a large feeling of the sky, of the light, and to mingle with the brown earth in its glistening glass, I cannot help believing that

my Indian ancestry had left deep in my being the legacy of its philosophy: the philosophy which speaks of fulfilment through a harmony with all things. For good or for evil such a harmony has the effect of arousing a great desire in us to seek our freedom, not in the man-made world but in the depth of the universe, and makes us offer our reverence to the divinity inherent in fire, water and trees, in everything moving and growing. The founding of my school had its origin in the memory of that longing for freedom, the memory which seems to grow beyond the skyline of my birth. Freedom in the mere sense of independence has no content, and therefore no meaning. Perfect freedom lies in the perfect harmony of relationship which we realise in this world—not through our response to it in *knowing* but in *being*. Objects of knowledge maintain an infinite distance from us who are the knowers. For knowledge is not union. Therefore the farther the world of freedom awaits us where we reach truth, not through feeling it by our senses, or knowing it by reason, but through the union of perfect sympathy.

—Rabindranath Tagore: "A Poet's School", L. K. Elmhirst: *Rabindranath Tagore: Pioneer in Education*, Visva-Bharati, 1961, pp. 51-52.

In the education of children, Tagore emphasises on freedom to have a fair role of the development of their sub-conscious mind which unfolds the religion of nurturing self-revelation. His main concern for the education of perfect sensitisation for the true religious spirit of mankind lies in how to allow every learner to have a deep and intimate association with the immediate environs so much so that the religion of creativity and critical consciousness may find the best avenues of effulgence in collaboration with Nature. For this education of *being* which is more than education of mere *knowing*, he approves education as a religion of self-respect and self-efflorescence which leads one towards fullness of education. As he poignantly asserts:

> Children have their active sub-conscious mind which, like the tree, has the power to gather its food from the surrounding atmosphere. For them the atmosphere is more important than rules and methods, building appliances, class teachings and text books. The earth has her mass of substance in her land and water. But, if I may be allowed figurative language, she finds here inspiration of freedom, the stimulation of her life, from her atmosphere. It is, as it were, the envelopment of her perpetual education. It brings from her depth responses in colours and perfume, music and movement, her incessant self-revelation, continual wonders of the unexpected. In his society man has the diffuse atmosphere of culture always about himself. It has the effect of keeping his mind sensitive to his racial inheritance, to the current of influences that come from tradition; it makes it easy for him unconsciously to imbibe he concentrated wisdom of aged. But in our educational organisations we behave like miners, digging only for thing substantial, through a laborious

> process of mechanical toil and not like a tiller of the soil, whose is in perfect collaboration with Nature, in a passive relationship of sympathy with the atmosphere.
>
> —*Ibid.*, pp. 63-64.

That learning the geography of foreign lands is less important than learning the history of human relationship is one of the most significant characteristics of Tagore's philosophy of education, which, indeed, disseminates the religion of man. He extends the horizon of learning the religion of man by means of having a close association with folk culture and tradition and making a direct endeavour at delving deep into the philosophy of transcendence as revealed in masters of folk songs. In fact, he is so impressed with the religion of love that he finds a great sense of delight in translating the folk songs of Jnanadas, where the religion of man finds one of the best avenues of effulgence:

> I had travelled all day and was tired; then I bowed my head towards thy kingly court still far away.
> Thy night deepened, a longing burnt in my heart
> Whatever the words I sang, pain cried through them—for even my songs thirsted....
> O my Lover, my Beloved, my Best in all the world.
>
> When time seemed lost in darkness, thy hand dropped in sceptre to take up the flute and strike the uttermost chords
> And my heart sang out,
> O my Lover, my Beloved, my Best in all the world.

> Ah, who is this whose arms enfold me?
> Whatever I have to leave, let me leave; and whenever I have to bear, let me bear
> Only let me work with thee,
> O my Lover, my Beloved, my Best in all the world.
>
> —Rabindranath Tagore: "An Indian Folk Religion", *Creative Unity,* Macmillan & Company Ltd., London, 1962, p. 89.

To seek 'my Best in the world' is that education which Tagore believes as the religion of all religions to be initiated into the world of the transcendence of love. This is an education which is a natural and spontaneous outcome of religious feelings, visions and sensibilities being baked in the warmth of transcendence as inherent in our folk songs of rich socio-cultural and religious moorings. Tagore himself has his religious vision from the lessons that he has learnt from a living and direct study of the mendicant religious sect of Bengal. As he frankly observes:

> It is needless to say........that I had neither the training nor the opportunity to study the mendicant religious sect in Bengal from ethnological standpoint. I was attracted to find out how the living currents of religious movements work in the heart of the people, saving them from degradation imposed by the society of the learned, of the rich, or of the high-born; how the spirit of man, by making use even of its have obstacles, reaches fulfilment, led thither, not by the learned authorities in the scriptures, or by the mechanical impulse of the

dogma-driven crowd, but by the unsophisticated aspiration of the loving soul. On the inaccessible mountain peaks of theology the snows of creed remain eternally rigid, cold, and pure. But God's manifest shower falls direct on the plain of humble hearts, flowing there in various channels, even getting mixed with some mud in its course, as it is soaked into the underground currents, invisible but ever-moving.

—*Ibid.*, p. 88.

The education of religious sensibilities which is, indeed, the education of introspective vision in the ends-in-view of ascent and transcendence can, as Tagore advocates, hardly be received through books. Rather is it an education of love born in living, loving and having the flora and fauna in and around as the great gifts of the All Beautiful. How to have such an education that simplifies and makes religion one's very own? Here is Tagore's answer in the words of music:

I seek Him alone who lives in my mind.
As He does exist,
Stars shine in the sky of my mind at night,
Flowers bloom in the forest in the morning.
As He does exist,
In the light of the stars of the eyes
There is so much of play of beauty and feast of colour in endless black and white.
As He remains with me,
The southern wind awakens my joy in my every limb,
His message is that is filled

In the tune of my song amid an unmindful *taan*,
He swings in me in the sweep of sorrow all of a sudden
He conceals Himself amidst work and makes me forget my work.
As eternal He is to me,
It is His gladness that at times filled in my moments.

—Rabindranath Tagore: *Gaan, Rabindra-Rachanavali,* Government of West Bengal, Calcutta, 1980, Vol. IV, p. 443.

[Translated by me]

Apart from making this self-revelation baked in the religion that Tagore has nurtured in his education of the philosophy of transcendence and ascent of man, he draws our attention to education that holds religion in reality and sustains the highest form of the spirit of self-dedication in quest of truth. This can be well elucidated by his invaluable address to the students at the Classic Theatre, Calcutta, more than a hundred years—on 17 *Chaitra* 1311 of the Bengali era:

> Devoid of reality, what with the mind or with the heart or even with imagination, there is the possibility of narrowness and deformity. Our patriotism proves this point. There is no connection between this well-being and the welfare of the country. The people of the country are dying of diseases, suffering from poverty and are being spoilt by non-education and ill education. Those who do not associate themselves with their endeavour whatsoever

to eliminate these ills imagine to have achieved by various improper imitation the bookish patriotism of foreign literature and history. For this, even after so many years, this patriotism failed to devote ourselves to admit sacrifice. The people of the country where people are not devoid of reality or not dependent on bookish education are really sacrificing their lives for the cause of the motherland. We can neither offer a little money nor do we spare a little time for her. We do not feel enthusiasm to know through the spirit of enquiry what our country actually is. Yoshida Torajiro was an eminent patriot of Japan. At the initial stage, by taking a little food with him, he gradually went on trekking the whole country on foot. Thus, by knowing the country most scrupulously, he thereafter engaged himself in teaching pupils. Towards the last stage, he had to sacrifice his life for the service of his country. The meaning of such a type of patriotism becomes revealing. When patriotism makes its foundation on the real knowledge and activities of the country, then alone it brings forth fruit like a tree that has its roots firmly stamped on the soil.

—Rabindranath Tagore: *Chhatrader Prati Sambhashan"* ("Address to the Students"), *Siksha,* Visva-Bharati, 1973, p. 23.

[Translated by me]

Tagore wants to impart religious education not in isolation from life and society but in total communion with one and all and with every item and experience that contributes to fullness of personality. Therefore, there is neither any scope for ritualism nor for dogmatism in his education for development of religious sensibilities.[1] As a matter of fact, he decries that education which pays rigorous attention to abstraction in carrying out some lifeless, mechanical and dull rules and regulations as ordained in scriptures without being responsive to what brings forth harmony and inner discipline in one's pursuit of truth, beauty, goodness, simplicity and other finer elements of poignancy and perfection. The education of religion is a thrilling, adventurous, unending and stimulating process where the vision of vastness beckons one to merge in the legion to be crystallised, chiselled and poignant in the promise of perfection. Tagore makes a very significant elucidation on this point:

> Religion is that institute of music where the father is teaching his son how to sing, wherc the tune of the soul is being transmitted from the Supreme Soul. It is not that music is being in total resonance everywhere in this institute of music. May be there is discord in tuning or *taal*. The sorrow to rectify this absence of tuning and *taal* in tunes and *taals* is very rude. In that rude sadness, the strings are torn apart many a time, but those are to be mended once again. The errors are not one and the same in case of everyone, nor are the constraints of equal nature in case of one and all. Someone is faulty in tuning. Somebody has limitations in *taal*. Again, someone is weak in both tuning and *taal*. This is why the pursuit is different but the end-in-view is the same. Everyone will have to have emancipation by stringing the

> instrument with the same pure tuning, by making the *alaap* with one pure *raagini* amidst the same pure joy where the significance of unison will be filled in with the symphony of instruments, vocal tunings, and hearts between the father and the son, the master and the disciple.
>
> —Rabindranath Tagore: *"Dharmer Artha", Sanchay, Rabindra-Rachanavali,* Government of West Bengal, Calcutta, 1992, Vol. XIV, p. 974.

[Translated by me]

With the ends-in-view of religion as above, Tagore wants to harmonise education with the finest principles and perspectives of making it available for one and all in the society so that the whole society rises up as one man in the pursuit of learning. Deeply pained with the role of education incapable of making a fruitful role in social cohesion by stringing the tunes for apposite symphony amongst all in the society, which would manifest the religion of man and society in diverse directions, he characteristically remarks:

> The word 'education' with which we are satisfied introspectively by pronouncing it has its appearance of the store-house; but, by looking outside, we encounter the sea of emptiness all around. The lofty lantern has been hung for the light of education in schools and colleges, but if that is a captured light in closed walls, then we would say that we are unfortunate. A picture manifests throughout

> the canvas. Likewise, in order to have explicitness, education awaits countrywide involvement. That education bereft of its extensive role is so vague and incomplete that its pains of poverty have died down in our mind due to our habits alone. When we compare our country with the other one in respect of education, we only observe the visible part and never make an account of the invisible one. With resemblance we see that there are also universities and their replicas in the forms of one or two are also being seen in our country. We forget that there is not a single fortunate country where beyond the stipulated educational institutions there is not a wider circumference well spread throughout the horizon of non-stipulated education embracing the whole society.
>
> —Rabindranath Tagore: *"Sikshar Vikiran"* (The Dissemination of Education"), *Siksha,* Visva-Bharati, 1973, p. 214.
>
> [Translated by me]

What prompts Tagore for appropriate dissemination of education amongst the *hoi polloi* is to introduce religion in the right manner and in the right direction. This is why he draws our attention to the invaluable contributions of the *toles* and the *chatuspathis* and dissemination of religious discourses through the *Ramayana* and the *Mahabharata* and other holy scriptures whereby religion never remains imprisoned in principles and regulations but verily becomes the way of life in day to day activities and thoughts. In this connection, his introspective vision of fusion between education and religion is significantly revealed as follows:

> Like the Mediaeval era in Europe, education through *sastras* alone was fundamental. The special pursuit of this education was made in *toles* and *chatuspathis,* but the role of learning was extended throughout the country. There was a continual exchange between specialised knowledge and general knowledge. There was not that antagonistic relationship between the assembly of scholars and the unscholarly locality as between an oasis and a desert. There was no part in the country that did not endear the *Ramayana,* the *Mahabharata*, the religious discourses that would regularly spread through diverse channels. Even those theoretical knowledge that are discussed under strenuous perseverance in philosophy were also irrigated in the soil of the minds of the masses all the time. The food for the tree needs to be made liquid so that the tree might take it in all its branches and twigs. In the same way, serious learning in those days has been simplified and disseminated among the minds of the masses. When public work was a part of religion in our country, the arrangements for reservoirs of water for every village were extensive by nature. To quench thirst, arrangements for water were spontaneously made by all together. There was no need for appealing to the spend-thrift personnel of the royal court for water. In the same way, society has disseminated indigenous learning in

> spontaneity. Otherwise, the whole country would turn into cruelly black barbarities. Learning then was not a property of the learned; that was a property of the whole society.
>
> —*Ibid.*, pp. 214-215.

[Translated by me]

An ardent connoisseur of the divine humanity, Tagore advocates education as the most meaningful and positive vehicle of religion. In fact, his very endeavour at educational experimentations in his own institution, Visva-Bharati, cater to the ideal of education for spiritual unity of all races—a crystallised vision of religion best exercised in the devoted pursuit of learning. His emphasis on education in an atmosphere of Nature with all her freedom, beauty and splendour affords within the learner a genuine urge to cultivate the finer spirit of religion.

The education thus nurtured in an atmosphere of Nature with her infinite contributions to one who is willing to learn the lesson of sympathy, love, co-operation and other components of fullness and elegance is the harbinger of the best possibilities for one's quest for religion par excellence. What Tagore aims at education for religious fulfilment in his own institution is significant:

> From the very beginning I tried to create an atmosphere which I consider to be more important than the class teaching. The atmosphere of Nature's own beauty was there waiting for us from time immemorial with her varied gifts of colours and forms, flowers and

fruits, with the joy of her mornings and the peace of her starry nights.

From the commencement of our work we have encouraged our children to be of service to our neighbours from which has grown up a village reconstruction work in our neighbourhood, unique in the whole of India. Round our educational work villages have grouped themselves in which the sympathy for nature and service for man have become one. In such an extension of sympathy and service, our mind realises its true freedom.

Along with this has grown an aspiration for even a higher freedom, freedom from all racial and national prejudice. Children's sympathy is often deliberately made narrow and distorted making them incapable of understanding alien people with different languages and cultures. This causes us, when our growing souls demand it, to grope after each other in ignorance, to suffer from the blindness of this age. The worst fetters come when children lose their freedom of heart in love.

We are building up our institution upon the ideal of the spiritual unity of all races. I hope it is going to be a great meeting place for individuals from all countries who believe in the divine humanity, and who wish to make atonement for the cruel disloyalty displayed against her by men.

I represent in my institution an ideal of brotherhood, where men of different countries

> and different languages can come together. I believe in the spiritual unity of man and therefore I ask the world to accept this task from me.
>
> —Rabindranath Tagore: "My Education a Mission", *The Modern Review,* Calcutta, June, 1931, pp. 622-623.

To welcome children to learn religion in its true perspectives of sensitivity, Tagore actually makes a 'home-coming' as he prefers to call it, for them in the world of Nature. The theoretical concepts of the different components of religion like sympathy, love, freedom, joy and others, all profoundly contributing to an enlightened and humane society become living and thrilling in close association with Nature who endears children with all the spirit of freshness and vigour. Tagore distinctly elucidates how he wants to infuse religion amongst children in the diversities of the mind and the heart:

> Children with the freshness of their senses come directly to the intimacy of this world. This is the first great gift they have. They must accept it naked and simple and never lose their power of quick communication. For our perfection we have to be at once savage and civilised; we must be natural with nature and human with human society.
>
> I wish I could say that we have fulfilled this dream in our school. We have only made a beginning; we have given the children an opportunity to find their freedom in nature by being able to love it. For love is freedom, it saves

us from paying with our soul for objects that are all too very cheap. I know men who preach the cult of the simple life by glorifying the spiritual merit of poverty. I refuse to imagine any special value in poverty when it is a mere negation. Only when the mind is sensitive to the deeper call of reality is it weaned away from the lure of the fictitious. It is callousness which robs us of our simple power to enjoy and dooms us to the indignity of snobbish pride in furniture and the foolish burden of expensive things. But to pit the callousness of asceticism against the callousness of luxury is to fight one evil with another, inviting the pitiless demon of the desert in place of the indiscriminate demon of the jungle.

With the help of literature, festive ceremonials and religious teachings I tried to develop in the children of my school their feeling for nature as also a sensitiveness to their human surroundings. I prepared for them a real homecoming into this world. among the subjects they learned in the open air, in the shade of trees, were music and painting, and they had their dramatic performances.

But this was not sufficient, and I waited for men and the means to be able to introduce into our school activities that would help build up character. I felt the need of the western genius for imparting to my educational ideal the strength which knew how to achieve a definite end of practical good.

—Rabindranath Tagore: "A Poet's School", *Towards Universal Man,* Asia Publishing House, Bombay, 1961, pp. 295-296.

Education under compulsion as it is very often manifested today is no education. It betrays the religion of self-askance and self-enquiry which are the true components of education for fullness. When education is caged and camouflaged in a mechanised process of observing some principles, it robs one of the freedom of action which is one of the most significant components that reveals the religion of education. Again, with freedom exercised in education, the creative consciousness of a learner finds the most favourable aura of efflorescence. When knowledge, action and creativity are designed and exercised in a sensitive and disciplined manner, education earns the glory of being in perfect accord with the religion of ceaseless realisation of the All Serene.

With the ends-in-view of education as above, Tagore cxplores and expands education in the direction of the religion of joy. That all education is the fountain of endless joy derived from, and in, freedom is an altogether new approach to realisation of the religion of the total development of man. It has three-fold approach to advancement in religion. First, there is a ceaseless endeavour in unification of knowledge, action and power. Second, the fullness of joy through education as one aims at, should have a crystallised vision of detachment which caresses religion in right order and ascent. Third, an unending involvement in and through education for realisation of the self is to be in unison with the Divine Self.

The education of freedom which is, indeed, the education of the self in the endless quest for the Divine

Self is what Tagore always identifies as true religion. It is this education which enables one to learn how to sacrifice oneself for the best cause of others and how to transcend oneself towards fullness.

To explore the real meaning of education as religion, Tagore emphasises on the education of the self best manifested in sacrifice and submission to whatever stands for excellence and transcendence. The genesis of freedom which is an invaluable component of education as he always maintains, is one's religion which stands for the ascent and excellence of the self. In his own words:

> The freedom of the seed is in the attainment of the *dharma,* its nature and destiny of becoming a tree; it is the non-accomplishment which is its prison. The sacrifice by which a thing attains its fulfilment is not a sacrifice which ends in death; it is the casting off of bonds which wins freedom.
>
> When we know the highest ideal of freedom which a man has, we know his *dharma,* the essence of his nature, the real meaning of his self. At first sight it seems that man counts that as freedom by which he gets unbounded opportunities of self-gratification and self-aggrandisement. But surely this is not borne out by history. Our revelatory men have always been those who have lived the life of self-sacrifice. The higher nature in man always seeks for something which transcends itself and yet is its deepest truth; which claims all its sacrifice, yet makes this sacrifice its own recompense. This is man's *dharma,* man's

> religion, and man's self is the vessel which is to carry this sacrifice to the altar.
>
> —Rabindranath Tagore: "The Problem of Self', *Sadhana,* Macmillan India Limited, New Delhi, Macmillan Pocket Tagore Edition, 1988, p. 62.

To make appropriate inroads to inner consciousness which always advocates what religion is and what it always ought to be is to make education the truest vehicle of religion. As an unparalleled visionary of education for fullness, Tagore expands the horizon of education by translating it as a religion of one's very own to be in unison of the religion of all. He also refers to the limitations of knowledge which cannot go beyond information and awaits the knowledge re-crystallised in joy and love for perfect unison with the All Serene. As he poignantly elucidates:

> Intellectual knowledge is partial, because our intellect is an instrument, it is only a part of us, it can give us information about things which can be divided and analysed, and whose properties can be classified, part by part. But Brahma is perfect, and knowledge which is partial can never be a knowledge of him.
>
> But he can be known by joy, by love. For joy is knowledge in its completeness, it is knowing by our whole being. Intellect sets us apart from the things to be known, but love knows its object by fusion. Such knowledge is immediate and admits no doubt. It is the same as knowing our own selves, only more so.

> Therefore, as the Upanishads say, mind can never know Brahma, words can never describe him; he can only be known by our soul, by her joy in him, by her love. Or, in other words, we can only come into relation with him by union—union of our whole being. We must be one with our Father, we must be perfect as he is.
>
> —*Ibid.,* pp. 136-137.

As health encapsulates the whole of one's physique, so is religion which encapsulates the whole of the human being, which is natural. Tagore advocates that natural and spontaneous efflorescence of religion where education shakes hands with the religion of wholeness—a journey endless and thrilling towards making an adventure in the fullness of man in perfection of wisdom and light. The prayer for such an education is: *Yadetat hridayang mama tadastu hridayang tava*—let thy heart be even as my heart is.

Do we solemnly share amongst ourselves that purity and poignancy in and through our education for religion and vice versa?

Reference

1. It is interesting to note in this connection how Swami Vivekananda comes closer to Rabindranath Tagore in explaining religion in terms of education and society:

> Religious ideas will have to become universal, vast, and definite, and then alone we shall have the fullest play of religion, for the power of religion has only just begun to manifest in the world. It is sometimes said that religion is dying out, that spiritual ideas are

dying out of the world. To me it seems that they have just begun to grow. The power of religion, broadened and purified, is going to penetrate every part of human life. So long as religion was in the hands of the chosen few or of a body of priests, it was in temples, churches, books, dogmas, ceremonials, forms and rituals. But when we come to the real, spiritual, universal concept, then and then alone religion will become real and living; it will come into our every nature, live in our every moment, penetrate every pore of our society, and be infinitely more a power for good than it has ever been before.

—Swami Vivekananda: "The Necessity of Religion", *The Complete Works of Swami Vivekananda,* Advaita Ashrama, Calcutta, Mayavati Memorial Edition, 1989, Vol.II, pp. 67-68.

10

Towards a Religion of Religions: Tagorean Forethoughts

Religion is a re-vision in a continual process of crystallisation. It is the very foundation of one's being always pining for the best effulgence of the All Serene within oneself. It seeks truth as truth is the existence of the All Serene awaiting the blending of love, joy, freedom, beauty, purity and perfection which prompt one in the recycling of whatever declares the glory of man.

Unlike any other thinker on religion, Rabindranath Tagore identifies and highlights religion as the truth of the Eternal Man. His quest for religion is, therefore, a quest for truth where man stands on the threshold of an eternal victory blessed with the crest of *Tat tamhosi*—Thou art that. It is a victory that speaks of the truth that comes out of the depths of freedom and creative impulse towards the beauty of awe and silence, humility and goodness, simplicity and vastness.

An iconoclast par excellence in the concept of religion, Tagore explores and advocates the religion of *ananda*—joy unending. It is a religion that unfolds the whole of one's being in the endless encounter with diverse experiences. With such a religion, Tagore himself presents us with the love that illumines and sparkles in the brilliance of silence:

> Ah, with pain do my words sink, sink down,
> In the flow of tears did I lose the tune!
> Your boat is on the water of the sea,
> On the shores do I roam about.
> Ah, no room for me in your golden boat—
> Where do I find the way in darkness?
> Ah, in desperation do my eyes pine away
> Towards the door do I stand and go on seeing!
> None tells me about the room where the lamp burns,
> Alone do I remain seated on the way
> On the sea-shore of the eternal night!
>
> —Rabindranath Tagore: *Gaan, Rabindra-Rachanavali,* Government of West Bengal, Calcutta, 1987, Vol. IV, No. 1126, p. 452.

[Translated by me]

Tagore makes religion wide open to embrace all the finer sentiments and softer feelings of mankind well assessed and re-assessed in terms of truth, beauty and goodness, modesty, simplicity and greatness. He does not enter into intricacies and dogmas in the name of religion nor does he allow himself to be lost in the melee of romantic self-consciousness. He admits the two entities of his own self—the one, the 'I' within himself and the other, the 'I' that embraces the family, the country, and the clime. But he pays more importance to the one who is within himself and who creates and re-creates everything in and around him. He is the All Serene who shows him the way to the greatest 'I'—the way to blissful emancipation. This is what Tagore describes as the religion of realisation of truth. This truth is the truth of *Paramatman,* the Supreme Soul—the truth that blesses us to encounter the Lord of life—*Jeevandevata.*

How does Tagore characterise his concept of religion? He simply asserts that he neither wants religion to be a matter of abstraction nor does he want to isolate himself from religion which he considers to be one's very own. When he speaks of religion as a very subjective matter, he does not simply leave it as a matter to be isolated. On the other hand, he glorifies it as *Jeevandevata* whom he endears as the heartiest of the heart.

Admittedly, Tagore makes us aware of the fact that his lectures in *The Religion of Man* are the outcome of a poet's religion expressed and baked in the effulgence and warmth of the consciousness of joy that paves avenues for emancipation of man. The fundamental point of departure he makes from from other visionaries of religion is that the realisation of the All Serene may be possible within one's own self—the self that represents *Jeevandevata.* He is the soul of the universal man. Therefore, whatever embodies the vastness of humankind represents the All Serene in effulgence of truth.

Tagore never wants religion to be dissociated from humankind. The mind of every human being has the infinite capacity to visualise the All Serene within himself and beyond himself. But the extinction of man from religion is simply a betrayal of the birth of man. Tagore has his own frank confession in this regard:

> Once sitting alone I was meditating in the very fashion of that self-extinction by tinkering

> with the ancient *mantras*. I had intended to flee away. It is not true that I did not achieve peace. Emancipation from agitation could have easily been available. In this way, I have been consoled at the time of sorrow. In this way, I have been released from temptation. Again, a day arrived when I admitted everything, accepted all. I saw that I am a part of that of the play going on amidst the dramatic stage of man. I visualised everyone by embracing everything. I would not say that this visualisation is a trivial one. This is also truth. To visualise life apart from *Jeevandevata,* the Lord of life, is to verily encounter sorrow, and to visualise the same in unison is to embrace emancipation.
>
> —Rabindranath Tagore: *"Manavsatya"*, ("The Truth of Man"), *Manusher Dharma* (The Religion of Man), *Rabindra-Rachanavali,* Government of West Bengal, Calcutta, 1992, Vol. XIV, p. 1049.

[Translated by me]

A serenely sensitive iconoclast in religious vision, Tagore heralds the glory of man in his march for encounter with the Lord of life. He treads towards a human goal divinised in the sense that divinity has its starting point not from the Lord but from man, and, with this vision of religion encompassing the human end-in-view, every success or failure of man in realisation of the All Serene has a strong bond of liability in terms of poignancy. Tagore himself advocates this religious poignancy in the form of a prayer:

> When I go from hence let this be my parting word, that what I have seen is unsurpassable.
>
> I have tasted of the hidden honey of this lotus that expands on the ocean of light, and thus am I blessed—let this be my parting word.
>
> In this playhouse of infinite forms I have had my play and here have I caught sight of him that is formless.
>
> My whole body and my limbs have thrilled with his touch who is beyond touch; and if the end comes here, let it come—let this be my parting word.
>
> — Rabindranath Tagore: *Gitanjali*, Macmillan India Limited, New Delhi, Macmillan Pocket Tagore Edition, 1988, No. XCVI, pp. 63-64.

For a religion of religions, Tagore makes an inner voyage unending but full of adventure, arduous but loving and serene, difficult but pleasant and full of the perfume of promise. The King of all kings as he attributes to the Innermost One emboldens him to weather all doubts and disbeliefs. He visualises the Lord of his heart as the Lord of all nuances he craves and pines for in quest of fullness.

The quest that Tagore makes in order to best encounter the Innermost One opens a new vista of religion where the essence of all religions converges for the unheard message of the heart and the unknown language of perfect tuning to herald the victory of the Man Eternal. He himself sets an example by making an extraordinary cohesion between the sky of his heart and that in Nature with all her marvels and splendour so much so that the meaning and the muse of religion find an altogether new platform of excellence:

> Every morning do I receive the pleasing touch of light
> The heavenly honour of existence
> The flow of blood is mingled with the current of lustre
> The message of light sounds in silence in body and mind
> With the palms of eyes stretched wide
> Upwards do I daily observe.
> The first reception of life is blessed with this light
> On the shore of the setting sun at the door of this light
> The last prayer of my life will be submitted.
> I think I speak in vain, all words are yet to be told.
> The message of the heart with that of the sky
> Is yet to be attuned with the perfect tuning
> The language to me has yet remained unknown.
>
> —Rabindranath Tagore: "*Rogasajyay*" ("On the Ailing Bed"), *Rabindra-Rachanavali,* Government of West Bengal, Calcutta, 1983, Vol. III, No. 32, p. 808.
>
> [Translated by me]

The canvas that Tagore portrays for a religion of religions is always simple but poignant. Here is a visionary of religion par excellence who earnestly aspires after visualising the real form of his own soul in the halo of the Sun, an abiding spokesman of the Great Unexpressed:

> Standing on the edge of the playground of creation
> At times do I visualise
> The other side of darkness
> Where mingled I was in the unending consciousness of the Great Unexpressed
> At this time of today's morning the words of saints do I recall
> Unfold, O Sun, unfold the cover of light.
> Let me see in the great halo of thy inmost heart
> The real form of my soul
> The I that adds its breath of life in the air at the day's end
> That ends its body in ashes.
> Let it not cast its shadow on the path of journey
> In disguise of truth
> In the playing arena on earth the taste of the nectar have I had in happiness and sorrow
> From time to time
> Time and again have I visualised the Endless behind the veil of the finite,
> Understood have I that the last meaning of this life was there
> In the form of that Beautiful
> In that muse unspeakable.
> When in the playhouse the doors would be wide open
> I would leave my salutation in the temple of the earth.
> Now offer those offerings of life
> That are valued beyond death.

—Rabindranath Tagore: *Janmadine* (*On the Birthday*), *Rabindra-Rachanavali*, Government of West Bengal, Calcutta, 1983, Vol. III, No. 13, p. 853.

[Translated by me]

What distinguishes Tagore in the concept of religion from other religious visionaries is that he never isolates religion from the way of life. Rather is he deeply involved in the religion of the inner man through outward manifestations and vice versa. This indicates the fact that from the standpoint of religious efflorescence he denounces 'a drunken ecstasy of emotion' and advocates religion as a process of evolution through exercise of reason and restraint in embracing the external universe. In his own words:

> Our partiality is for the internal world. we would cast aside with contumely the field of power and of extension. We would realise Brahma in meditation only in his aspect of completeness, we have determined not to see him in the commerce of the universe in his aspect of evolution. That is why in our seekers we so often find the intoxication of the spirit and its consequent degradation. Their faith would acknowledge no bondage of law, their imagination soars unrestricted, their conduct disdains to offer any explanation to reason. Their intellect, in its vain attempts to see Brahma inseparable from his creation, works itself stone-dry, and their heart, seeking to confine him within its own outpourings, swoons in a drunken ecstasy of emotion. They have not

> even kept within reach any standard whereby they can measure the loss of strength and character which manhood sustains by thus ignoring the bonds of law and the claims of action in the external universe.
>
> —Rabindranath Tagore: "Realisation in Action", *Sadhana,* Macmillan India Limited, New Delhi, Macmillan Pocket Tagore Edition, 1988, pp. 107-108.

Earlier Tagore has made an exquisite elucidation by means of making a comparative study between the body and the soul to prove the point that in our realisation of Brahma, our quest should be both internal and external:

> It is the very characteristic of life that it is not complete within itself; it must come out. Its truth is in the commerce of the inside and the outside. In order to live, the body must maintain its various relations with the outside light and air—not only to gain life-force, but also to manifest it. Consider how fully employed the body is with its own inside activities; its heart-beat must not stop for a second, its stomach, its brain, must be ceaselessly working. Yet this is not enough; the body is outwardly restless all the while. Its life leads it to an endless dance of work and play outside; it cannot be satisfied with the circulations of its internal economy, and only finds the fulfilment of joy in its outward excursions.
>
> The same with the soul. It cannot live on its own internal feelings and imaginings. It is

ever in need of external objects; not only to feed its inner consciousness but to apply itself in action, not only to receive but also to give.

The real truth is, we cannot live if we divide him who is truth itself into two parts. We must abide in him within as well as without. In whichever aspect we deny him we deceive ourselves and incur a loss. *Brahma has not left me, let me not leave Brahma.* If we say that we would realise him in introspection alone and leave him out of our external activity, that we would enjoy him by the love in our heart, but not worship him by outward ministrations; or if we say the opposite, and overweight ourselves on one side in the journey of our life's quest, we shall alike totter to our downfall.

—*Ibid.*, pp. 105-106.

For a journey of our life's quest for the religion of religions as Tagore thinks and experiments, one cannot but enrich the emptied life in the ocean of deepest fullness. The beckoning is there eternal and thrilling from within and from outside, but who responds in all serenity and poignancy? As Tagore murmurs the words of prayer:

When the heart is hard and perched up, come upon me with a shower of mercy.
When grace is lost from life, come with a burst of song.
When tumultuous work raises its din on all sides shutting me out from beyond, come to me, my lord of silence, with thy peace and rest.
When my beggarly heart sits crouched, shut up in a corner, break open the door, my king, and come with the ceremony of a king.

When desire blinds the mind with delusion and dust, O thou holy one, thou wakeful, come with thy light and thy thunder.

—Rabindranath Tagore: *Gitanjali,* Macmillan India Limited, New Delhi, Macmillan Pocket Tagore Edition, 1988, No. XXXIX, pp. 22-23.

Do we join the prayer to best explore the religion of religions?

Reference

1. Professor Sisirkumar Ghose makes a very significant observation on the Poet's religion:

To move towards a truly human goal, we need a centre of unity and relationship, a shared heritage for the family of Man. This means an end to rivalries between nations and ideologies, the positing of some universal ethics, a transcendent humanity. Along with other teachers, past and present, Tagore has pointed out how the obsession wth the "little self", contingent and conditioned, hampers the human whole. The consciousness of our unity with all-that-is (*Sarvamidam)* may be religion's only ground and rationale. Man's physical body is born and dies; his transcendent humanity, his true being, is for ever. So runs the poetic gospel, Tagore's variation on Advaita. Who can deny its appeal?

The spiritual unity of life and aspiration is Tagore 's métier and mainstay. All else, theology, legislation seems secondary. What it adds up to, then, is this: to be religious one must be sensitive. Though he does not say so, not in so many words, only for the Poet can there be religion as lived life, *Lebenswelt.* That such an attitude overly aesthetic, and personalist, might also reveal an allergy towards the 'trivial plane', the everyday life and common man, is not surprising. In this undiscovered self no man is quite common. Souls that do not aspire are god's failure.

—Sisirkumar Ghose: "A Poet's Religion", *Rabindranath Tagore,* Sahitya Akademi, New Delhi, 1986, p. 86.

Index

D

E

F

S

T

U

V

W

Y